Winning At Customer Services And Call Centre Job Interviews

Including answers to the interview questions

By Annette Lewis and Joe McDermott

Publishers Note

First published in Great Britain in 2006 by Anson Reed Limited.

First edition 2006

Anson Reed Limited
145-157 St Johns Street,
London EC1V 4PY
United Kingdom

© Anson Reed Limited 2006

The publisher makes no representation, express or implied, with regard to accuracy of the information in this book and cannot accept any legal responsibility for any error or omissions that may be made.

British Library Cataloguing in Publication Data
A CIP Record for this book is available from the British Library
ISBN 0-9552629-4-1

Cover Design: Diogo Garcia

About the Author

Annette Lewis is an experienced HR professional having worked for many years within the Customer Services and Banking Industries. She has most recently acted as recruiting manager with the Health Service where she was instrumental in introducing interviewing best practice procedures and in training managers and staff. She is currently pursuing a successful career as a job and lifestyle coach

Joe McDermott is a qualified professional with almost 15 years experience and has held senior management positions in the US and Europe. He has managed teams of up to 150 people and is an experienced interviewer, job coach and career consultant.

Table of Contents

Introduction

Flexible working, attractive remuneration packages, a wide variety of opportunities working within a vast range of industries all go towards making Customer Services one of the most popular choices for many people looking for a long term career. Open any newspaper or search on the internet and you will come across thousands of jobs ranging from Call Centre Agents, Advisors, Supervisors, right up to Call Centre Managers and Heads of Customer Services. It is an attractive career option and it is a competitive one and this guide is designed to greatly improve your chances of success whether you are looking for your first job, moving up the career ladder or changing jobs into the Customer Services sector.

About Us

We consider the job interview to be the most important part in the job search process. It really is make or break and could be the culmination of months of effort on your part. You may have spent time creating a powerful CV or Resume, researching a variety of companies, applying for a number of jobs and been through the agency or application process. Finally you have an invite to attend an interview and the last thing to do at this stage is make some small mistake which loses you the job and puts you back at square one.

This guide has been written by senior managers, all of whom have extensive experience of the Customer Services and Call Centre industries. We have interviewed for a range of positions from entry level up to head of department in a variety of companies in Banking, Finance, Health, Entertainment, Sales, Manufacturing and Hospitality. We know what works and does not work in the interview room and having been interviewed many times ourselves, we know exactly how it feels from both sides of the desk. We have combined all our learning into this volume and provide all the essential information you will need to win in any job interview.

About this Book

The secret to giving a great interview performance is to prepare properly and this is true no matter how experienced you are. It will help reduce any nervousness you may feel, it will let you step into the interviewer's shoes and understand exactly what they are looking for when they ask you a question and very importantly it will help you answer the question, is this job and company right for me?

1

Anticipating the questions you will be asked, practicing winning answers, following all the guidelines on what to do, how to act and what to wear are key to a successful outcome and in this guide we address all of these. We provide all the information you need, starting with an analysis of the Customer Services and Call Centre industries, the skills required and the types of jobs available. We discuss the theory behind job interviews, what the interviewer is looking for and the different format of interview you will encounter.

We show you how to prepare properly, how to predict the questions and how to carry out a mock interview. We help you choose the right clothes and the right words to make a great first impression and we teach you the key actions required to keep you at the forefront of the interviewers mind when they are making their decision.

The interview is a two way dialogue and we teach you how to answer any interview question, what to say and not to say to convince the interviewer you are the right person for the job. We provide model answers to 96 questions asked at Customer Services and Call Centre job interviews including competency and behavioural questions and questions specific to the common jobs found in Customer Services. Rather than repeating these answers word for word however, we recommend that you use them as a guide to help in formulating your own replies in your own words. By doing so, you will come across much more smoothly and naturally.

We have included four interview scripts, one each for a Customer Services Advisor role, Call Centre Agent, Customer Care Team Leader and Head of Customer Services. These have been used in actual interviews and are perfect for use in a mock interview.

How to Use this Book

This book is designed in such a way that it can be read either from cover to cover or used as a reference whereby the reader can dip into any part or section as required. We use a number of icons in the guide and recommend that you make careful note when you see these displayed.

Hot Tips	Warning	Action	Key Learning

Chapter 1

All about Customer Services and Call Centres

Almost all modern organisations have some form of Customer Service function which can range from the receptionist who meets and greets visitors up to a dedicated call centre with 1,000's of employees. The activity of Customer Service refers to the behaviours and actions an organisation undertakes during its interaction with its customers and can be present at all times, before, during and after a transaction. The task of the Customer Service function is to make this interaction as easy and smooth as possible, generating goodwill and in turn encouraging loyalty and repeat purchases.

With the rising dominance of the service sector in the global economy, Customer Service has grown in importance over the past 20 years as its impact on individuals, households, firms, and societies has become widespread. In the UK the Call Centre industry has grown by over 250% and is forecast to have 1m employees by 2007. It is a key part of the economic structure and provides excellent career opportunities at all levels.

Careers in Customer Services

A career in Customer Services can certainly be rewarding. While some may find the task of dealing with people stressful, for many others there is a sense of achievement in 'helping' and making sure that customers get what they want. Many jobs are specifically 'customer facing' which refers to the situation where the customer is being interacted with directly, for example in the branch of a bank or over the telephone or internet. In addition, there are many different Customer Service roles where the employee never has to deal directly with the customer. For example, when processing a credit card application, the front end sale may have been completed in a live environment with a sales agent, after which the application is sent to a processing centre where the details are input into a computer and credit reference checks performed. Even though this individual never sees the customer, they are still part of the customer service chain.

The Customer Service industry job listings are wide-ranging and encompass many sectors including, Banking and Financial Services, Travel and Entertainment, Insurance, Government and Local Authorities, the Health Service and Utilities such as Gas and Electrical providers. In fact any organisation which deals with customers will have a Customer Services function of some description. Jobs will be advertised under Call or Contact Centre, Customer Care, Customer Support, Line Support, Order Processing, Sales and Sales Support, Technical Support, Telecoms, Telesales, Account Management, Complaints Support, General Enquiries etc. Sometimes there is no mention at all of Customer Service in the job title but nevertheless Customer Service is what the job is mainly about, for example, Receptionist or Travel Agent Clerk.

At entry level, the most common job titles you will come across include:

- Customer Services Advisor
- Call Centre Agent
- Customer Service Assistant
- Customer Service Representative
- Customer Care Consultant
- Customer Service Administrator
- Customer Support
- Customer Co-ordinator
- Sales and Telesales Agent
- Receptionist/Switchboard Agent

All of these are starting positions and in this guide we will classify these under **Customer Services Advisor (CSA).** The functions of the role may include dealing with sales or payment queries, complaints, change of address, questions about a product or service, pre and post sales support and management of customer records. In reality the variety of activity involved is vast with some tasks common to all roles and others specific to the recruiting company or industry.

The next level is **Team Leader or Supervisor** and these may be seen advertised as:

- Customer Action Team Leader
- Call Centre Team Leader
- Customer Services Supervisor
- Telesales Team Leader
- Collections Team Leader

Their function is to manage a group of Customer Service Advisors (CSA) and within a call centre function this will usually be between 10 and 15. They will be responsible for supervising, coaching, motivating and developing the team and ensuring that staff rotas are maintained, targets are communicated and met and agents have adequate training to do so. They may also have to handle customer servicing calls or contacts which have been 'escalated' from a CSA.

If the customer services function is large enough there may be another level called **Customer Service Managers.** These middle managers are often referred to as Performance Managers or Team Managers and look after a number of supervisors or team leaders and may be in charge of a department such as Complaints or Sales.

At the top there will be an overall management team led by the **Head of Customer Services.** This post may also be referred to as:

- Contact Centre Manager
- Call Centre Director
- Sales Manager

Running alongside the core Customer Services Team will be support functions including Technical and IT, Marketing, Financial, Human Resources and Training. While these functions are essential to making sure that the department runs properly, in this guide we concentrate on the core Customer Services roles as mentioned above.

Skills Required in Customer Services

The variety of skills required to work in Customer Services depends largely on how complex the job is. Some roles will require selling skills or technical ability, while many others don't. Generally, excellent customer service is provided by individuals who are interested in people, understand their needs and are able to work consistently and reliably to meet their requirements.

As the demand for customer service skills continues to grow many employers have cited that there is a lack of suitably skilled staff to fill available vacancies. They have listed the following as essential and desirable competencies that an ideal candidate should possess.

- Excellent communication
- Customer handling
- Interpersonal Skills
- Keyboard and computer skills
- Problem solving
- Planning and organising
- Team working
- Understanding customer needs
- Ability to follow procedures
- Showing initiative

In addition, the employee would need to have a good knowledge of the organisation's products and services and the systems used to deliver these to customers. This information will be provided during the initial training or induction period however we recommend that a job interview candidate should have made some effort to learn the basic details about the company and its products prior to the interview.

Most organisations provide their own specialist in-house Customer Service training programmes and in addition for someone considering a career in Customer Services some form of outside training may be beneficial. Further information can be obtained by:

- contacting your local college of further education
- contacting your local Chamber of Commerce or town council
- viewing the Learn Direct website or other online training

When looking at a career in Customer Services and wondering which jobs to apply for, the key points you need to consider are:

- Whether you enjoy the process of dealing with people
- Do you want to have direct face-to-face contact with customers such as in retail sales, hotels, bank branches and receptionists?
- Do you prefer contact with customers over the phone or via the internet, working in a contact centre?
- Would you like a role which is not dealing with customers directly but part of the process such as in a banking back office?

There is a multitude of roles available in this industry and the work can be varied and flexible with many organisations now operating flexi-time allowing staff to work different shift patterns to suit their personal lives.

The Labour Market

It is estimated that there are 20,000 call centres in the USA employing up to 2m people. In the UK the figure is 5,500 call centres employing 400,000 agents and predictions are that the UK could have 7,000 call centres employing 1m people including support functions by 2007. It follows that a career in Customer Services is a long term and sustainable option and opportunities for development are limitless. Salaries can vary depending on the location and type of work however typical Customer Services remuneration in contact centres is:

Customer Services Advisor (CSA)
Range: $20,000 - $22,500 US / £11,800 - £13,000 UK
Sales agents: £17,600 average (including commissions)

Team Leader
Average: $33,000 US - £19,500 UK

Team Manager
Average: $40,000 US - £23,900 UK

Head of Customer Service / Call Centre Manager
Average: $62,000 US - £36,900 UK

Call Centre Director
Average: $105,500 US- £63,100 UK

Source: UK and US Salary surveys 2005

Key Issues Facing the Industry

It is quite common to come across a question in the interview such as 'What do you know about the Customer Services Industry?' and in this section we consider the key challenges which the industry is facing. By demonstrating some knowledge of these you will reassure the interviewer that you are serious about the job and about your career in this sector. The industry has grown considerable over the past 15 years and now over 2m people are employed in 20,000 call centres in the USA and over 400,000 agents in 5,500 call centres in the UK. The key issues as identified by call centre managers are:

High Staff Turnover:
This is a common feature of many Call Centres and has been reported at an average of 25% annually although it can run to over 30% especially in areas where there is a high density of Call Centres located. This is evident in Coventry in the UK where many of the large banks have their call centres and in Phoenix, Arizona in the US where companies such as AMEX, JP Morgan and Bank One are located.

Availability of Skilled Resources:
There is a shortage of skilled workers including management who can deal with customers effectively and this is made worse by the high level of staff turnover in the industry as mentioned above.

Cost Containment:
This is always a challenge for large and small organisations alike.

Changing Technology:
Companies have to continuously invest in new systems and equipment in order to keep up with competition and to provide the best service to its customers.

Targets:
All Call Centres will have targets in terms of call answer rates, number of complaints, customer satisfaction, sales and turnover and these are becoming more difficult to achieve. All this adds pressure to the staff involved exacerbating the high level of attrition.

Outsourcing to India and Asia:
Many banks and insurance companies have been opening Contact Centres in Asia and in India particularly. A combination of skilled labour and low wages allows the organisation to complete the same tasks at a fraction of the cost.

What makes Good Customer Service?

To be able to work efficiently in a Customer Services environment it is essential that an employee knows what good Customer Service is. They must be able to differentiate between a good and bad experience and an interviewer will ask questions designed to discover the candidates ability to identify both.

Many of us have come across poor Customer Service whether we realised it or not. Maybe we purchased a product which did not live up to its description or took longer to arrive than expected. Maybe it did not work and when we called to complain we had to wait in a telephone queue for many minutes. When we finally got through we may have been met with an unresponsive agent who did not understand what we wanted or were unable to help. Maybe they did not do what they said they were going to do or they gave us the run-around. All of the above constitutes a poor customer experience and a lack of proper Customer Service.

Here are some key pointers in terms of what makes good Customer Service:

Easy to Contact

It should be easy for a customer to contact the Customer Service department with telephone numbers, emails and fax numbers readily available. They should be open when the customer needs them and ideally for 24 hours a day, 7 days per week.

Quick Response

A standard indicator in the call centre industry is that 80% of calls should be answered within 20 seconds. This suggests that 20% are not and in an ideal situation we suggest that the target should be 99% within 20 seconds and ideally within 3 rings. Similarly, emails should be answered within 24 hours.

Listening and Understanding

A key skill for a Customer Service Advisor is the ability to listen. Very often the customer just wants to get it off their chest and be heard and may not require any additional services.

Stay Calm

Very often a customer will be angry when they get through and it is vital that the agent remains calm and in control. A good agent will be able to listen, empathise and agree a solution without compromising the company.

Make the customer feel special

This follows on from the previous two points and involves treating the customer with respect, allowing them to talk and validating their comments or complaints.

Do what you say you will

If you agree a plan of action with the customer, for example to exchange faulty goods or send out an application form, it is vital that this is done within the timeframe agreed.

Below, we list some key words which can be used when describing good Customer Service and which can be used when formulating your interview answers. We have analysed these into four categories as follows:

Staff:	Products	Convenience	Environment
Friendly, Understanding, Good listener, Efficient Helpful, Courteous Empathetic Knowledgeable, Accurate, Resourceful, Empowered Trustworthy, Reliable Responsible	Good selection Good quality Available immediately Clear descriptions Clear pricing Competitive prices	Convenient locations and opening hours Fast service Self-service Quick and easy checkout Shipping/delivery Installation Phone/web support Easy return policy	Modern Clean Organised Safe

Business Process Outsourcing (BPO)

A relatively recent trend which started in the mid to late 90's but has escalated over recent years is the outsourcing of non-core activities to specialist companies. The theory is that the outsourcing organisations can focus on what they do best, be it manufacturing or selling and leave the servicing of the customers to someone else who is better. Benefits of this strategy include reduced cost and improved customer service.

The most common business process that gets outsourced is Customer Services especially those through Call Centres and IT help desks. US companies have outsourced to India and other Asian countries and are now moving services to Latin America especially Costa Rica where there are approximately 500,000 call centre workstations. A nearness to head office and the ability to speak Spanish and English is an attraction that suggests high growth in the industry in Nicaragua, El Salvador, Panama and Costa Rica over the coming years. Dell, Western Union and Proctor and Gamble have all outsourced some functions to some of these countries.

UK organisations which have followed this trend include Barclays Bank, HSBC, Norwich Union, BT and Tesco with most outsourcing to India. A quality pool of educated people, high levels of spoken English, good technological infrastructure all make this the destination of choice. At present in India, Business Process Outsourcing (BPO), the technical term for call centres is a £1.7bn industry. It has grown by 60% a year since 2000, and employs 260,000 people, with the rest of Asia accounting for another 50,000 offshore jobs.

Eastern Europe and North Africa are also developing as destinations for outsourcing. The Czech Republic, Poland and Hungary will be the destination of choice for higher-end jobs for German and English-speaking customers while Romania and Bulgaria are expected to focus on routine queries.

Prospects for the BPO industry are favourable with more than half of the 500 BPO companies in India's Silicon Valley, Bangalore, expected to increase their employee base by 20-40% over the next 12-18 months. A major problem however is high turnover rates sometimes as high as 50%. In Chapter 12 we pose some questions which may be asked of candidates interviewing for BPO positions.

Glossary of Terms

For those new to the Customer Services industry there may be many new words in this guide and in this section we give an explanation of the most commonly used.

Call Centre / Contact Centre: A department or office where calls and other forms of contact such as emails from customers are dealt with. There may be specialist teams dealing with different types of contacts such as sales, complaints, payments etc.

Telemarketing / Telesales: The activity of selling over the phone, either when the customer has called a specific number or by 'cold calling' where the agents calls the customer directly.

Customer Facing: A customer facing role is one which directly interacts with the customer either face-to-face or via the telephone, email or post.

Inbound Call: Call received in the Call or Contact Centre

Outbound Call: Call made by the agent to the customer

Customer Relationship Management (CRM): Refers to the activity of managing customers and includes customer servicing as well as maintaining databases and contact with the customer either for marketing or servicing purposes.

Staff Turnover: Also known as staff attrition, this is the rate at which employees leave the company to find another job.

Outsourcing: Refers to moving a process or function to another country, i.e. located 'offshore'. Links are usually maintained to the original country.

IVR System: Interactive Voice Response system is one which uses touch tone dialling to interact with the customer. An automated voice will ask the caller to press a number for a particular service.

Chapter 2

Customer Services and Call Centre Job Interview Basics

For anyone interested in working in the Customer Services industry, a job interview is inevitable. They are used by almost all organisations irrespective of size or industry and can range from a full day spent in an assessment centre to a presentation in front of the Board of Directors depending on the level or type of job being recruited for. There is no way we can think of to escape the job interview process and in fact we consider it to be the most important part in your job search.

So what exactly is a job interview? Many candidates have likened it to an audition for a part in a play, others regard them as painful interrogations and some industry gurus suggest that they are a waste of time. In fact they can be all of the above but essentially we see a job interview as a complex interaction between two parties both of whom are offering something while simultaneously seeking to have a need met.

Purpose of an Interview

An interview is a two way process. On the one hand the interviewer is seeking information from you which will allow them to make a correct decision but you are also learning from the interviewer and most importantly deciding if in fact this job is right for you. You may end up spending many years of your life with an organization and it is vital that you too make the right choice.

A vacancy in the recruiting organization triggers the process. This can be due to the previous job holder leaving or it may be a new position that has been created. Either way, there is a **'NEED'** that has been identified which is the requirement for someone to fill the vacancy. The recruiter will certainly be under pressure to fill the position with a suitably qualified person and they may need to find someone reasonably quickly. They are busy people, their time may be limited and in reality they are keen to recruit the best person in the minimum amount of time. To attract the right person, they recruiter will be making an **'OFFER'**. This will be made up of the salary and benefits, working environment, promotion prospects, training, career development and security among others.

For a potential multitude of reasons, you are in the job market and are looking for work. You too have a **'NEED'**. You have a set of requirements and are looking for a position which will satisfy your needs, be they financial, advancement, status or power. You are making an **'OFFER'** to the recruiter which consists of your skills, experience, mental and physical abilities and presence.

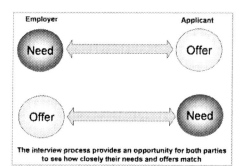

The interview process provides an opportunity for both parties to see how closely their needs and offers match

The reason for the interview process is to see how well these 'needs' and 'offers' match and the interview itself is an actual conversation whereby both parties are trying to find out if the others offering will satisfy their need. Ultimately both parties are looking to make the right decision.

To be in control in an interview situation it is essential that you understand this basic rationale for the interview. Once you do, you will be better placed to analyse what the recruiting organisation is looking for and 'sell' yourself accordingly. In addition, by remembering that it is a two way process and you are offering something valuable which the recruiter needs will put you in a position of strength and confidence.

What Every Interviewer Is Looking For

Irrespective of the job, the company, the level or type of position being recruited for, there are three requirements the interviewer is seeking answers to. We call these the 3Cs:

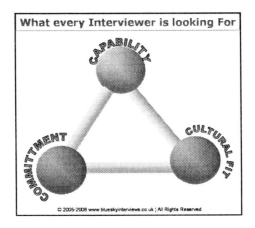

Capability: Are you able to do the job. From your CV/Resume the interviewer already believes the answer to this question is YES and their task is to check and validate this belief during the interview.

Commitment: Will you do the job and will you stay with the company. The interviewer does not want to have to repeat the recruitment process within at least the next two years.

Cultural Fit: Will you fit with the company, the team and the recruiting manager in terms of personality, chemistry, values and styles.

Having this knowledge will help greatly in anticipating the questions and in formulating winning answers.

Interview Styles

In Chapter 3 we look in detail at the different types of interview you will come across and in this section we consider the different styles an interviewer may use. The style chosen will determine how the questions are phrased and in which order and an interviewer may actually use a combination of styles during the interview. Once you know and understand the different styles you will be able to stay in control and tailor your answers accordingly.

Directional

Using this style the interviewer asks specific direct questions in a pre-set order and the interview feels very structured. It does not allow the candidate to veer greatly from the direction the interviewer wants to go and even if a very interesting 'hook' is thrown by the candidate the interviewer may not respond. The reason for this is that the company wants to maintain a great degree of consistency from one interview to the next and so make the selection process easier and fairer. This is generally used in large organisations which have heavy recruitment loads with many managers interviewing for the same type of role. You would typically encounter this style in interviews for Call Centre Agents and Customer Service Advisors.

Non-Directional

Generally, this style is used for higher level recruitment and feels more like a conversation. The interviewer will use open language and questioning and will give a greater degree of control to the candidate. They will be asked leading and probing questions and will be given the opportunity to elaborate on answers and give information not asked for directly. We would expect this style to be adopted in higher level appointments such as Customer Service Team Leaders and Supervisors and Head of Department.

Behavioural

This refers more to the format of questioning, is more often used in conjunction with the previous two styles and may take up 25% of the total interview time. This is used as a tool for the interviewer to discover how your past performance in a previous role may contribute to the role being recruited for. The interviewer will ask open-ended questions relating to your behaviour in past situations and will try to match this with the pre-set requirements of the role.

Behaviour based questions require you to provide specific examples of what you have done in the past and usually take the form of:

Tell me about a time when you....
Give an example of a situation you found yourself in and what did you do...
Describe a situation which caused you problems and how you resolved it...

We will come across these types of questions later and in answering suggest that you are specific, concise, honest and positive. Always remember that the interviewer is looking to answer the 3Cs.

Presentation

Quite often and especially with senior appointments such as Head of Customer Services or Contact Centre Manager the candidate may be expected to give a presentation usually as part of an interview and often to a panel.

If you are asked to give a presentation as part of your interview phone and check on the equipment that will be made available on the day. Do remember to bring a back up which can be on a memory stick or hard copy.

If you arrive and find that the room and equipment are not set up as you expected or were told, do not panic. You may find that this is a test to see how you re-act under pressure. Use your hard copy back-ups and carry on with your presentation as normal.

Chapter 3

Interview Formats

The format that is used to conduct the interview will be dependent on many factors. The training and preference of the interviewer, the type of organisation offering the job, for example government or private, the policy of the Human Resources department, the seniority of the position being recruited for, all will have an input into the type of interview used. Indeed for more senior positions it is quite common to experience more than one interview format during the recruitment process.

For example, you may firstly have to attend an assessment centre and complete psychometric tests which can be followed by an interview with the HR department prior to making a presentation to a panel of interviewers. In this chapter we will look at the different interview formats you will encounter within the Customer Services and Call Centre industries, including one-on-ones, panel interviews and round robins and we give advice and tips on how best to succeed in each.

The most common formats used when recruiting for Customer Service roles are One-on-Ones, Telephone Interviews and Panel Interviews. In addition, it is becoming increasingly common for candidates to attend an Assessment Centre and to complete Psychometric Tests. It is important that you know which type of interview format is being used from very early on in the process so that you can prepare properly and a telephone call to the recruiting organisation or to the agency if one is involved should elicit this information.

One on One's

This is the most common type of interview you will come across and involves one interviewer and one candidate. Initially your first meeting may be with a Human Resource representative who will effectively screen you for the role and make sure that certain basic requirements are in place. They will not be particularly interested or knowledgeable about the technical or day to day side of the role and will probably not ask any detailed questions regarding Capability, but will be more interested in Commitment and Cultural Fit.

They will also be keen to determine if you show integrity and honesty and may be looking for a fit based on diversity and equality guidelines. They will also ask questions about your previous job, reasons for leaving, salary and benefits and may ask about your salary expectations for the job you applied for.

Having met someone from the HR function, the next stage of the interview process will be with the individual who is hiring for the role. This person is likely to be your new boss and may be a person you will be spending a lot of time with in the future. Now is the time to find out if you think you will get on or not. It is this individuals' needs you are trying to match your offer to and at the same time you are looking to determine if what they are offering fits your own needs. They will be interested in all 3Cs, Capability, Commitment and Cultural Fit and their questions as we shall see later will be targeted towards answering these. By understanding this and the interviewer's perspective you will be able to anticipate and prepare for the kinds of questions someone in their position may ask.

If you are invited for an initial meeting with the Human Resources department do remember to treat this as you would any other interview. They have got the power to eliminate you from the process before you have a chance to see anybody else.

Round Robin

This is a series of one on one interviews whereby the candidate moves from one interviewer to another over the course of a couple of hours. For example the first interview may be with the Human Resource representative, followed by the supervisor or team leader and this may be finished up with a shorter interview with a senior director or manager who will give the overall ok. The questions may vary slightly but ultimately they will all be seeking to see if you fit with the 3Cs and your interview question and answer practice as detailed later will ensure that you will be able to impress at each meeting.

Panel Interviews

This involves two or more representatives interviewing the candidate at the same time. Typically, the panel would include the individual you will be working for, a Human Resources representative, possibly a senior manager or team member and if the job was within a government department an independent assessor would sit in. This format can be quite daunting for many people however the key point to remember is not to treat this any differently to a standard one-on-one. The questions will be the same, the structure will be the same, the only variant is the participants may play roles such as the aggressor, the interrupter, the observer.

The key to success in this type of interview is to make eye contact with the person asking the question but briefly address the whole panel when answering and then finish up making eye contact with the questioner when finished.

If someone is being aggressive, remember that this may be a role they are asked to play. It is not a personal attack and is designed to see how you react under pressure.

If you are interrupted while giving an answer, stay calm and acknowledge the question or comment but ensure that you have answered the original question sufficiently by saying "Good question but before I answer I would just like to add in reply to the previous question that....."

Treat a silent member of the panel as all others and when appropriate you could direct one of your questions to them.

Telephone Interviews

A telephone interview may be used by an organisation for a number of reasons. You may have been networking and the company wants to touch base and get a feel for what you can offer, you may have sent out your CV /Resume with an application and they want to check some details, either the employer or agency may be going through an initial screening process, there may be distance restrictions whereby a department or company executive who has the final say may be based overseas. Irrespective of the reason you must be prepared and always treat this "informal chat" as a proper interview. Sometimes you will have prior knowledge of the interview and have agreed a time and date. Quite often you will have a call when you least expect and it can come during an awkward moment. You should be asked if it is convenient to talk and if not, say so and while not ideal you can agree an alternative time and day. You can turn this into a positive by saying that you are glad they called; you are very interested in the position/company and would be delighted to talk further. You could explain that you are, for example, about to make a presentation, close a meeting, finish with a client etc.

Guidelines for Telephone Interviews

Be prepared
To do this we recommend that you keep a file containing your CV or Resume, details of the jobs you have applied for and the relevant company details close to the telephone.

Stay calm
If you are surprised and caught unawares, stay calm, be positive and friendly and say 'I'm glad you called and would be delighted to talk. Can you hold on a moment while I close the door/pop into my office?' This will give you a minute to put the kids into another room, get the file to hand and take a few deep breaths.

Switch off
If you had a TV or radio on, if you were cooking or if any machinery is working in the background then switch them off.

Smile
While the caller cannot see you they will detect this in the quality of your voice. In addition, you will feel better and more positive and this will also come across to the caller.

Walk about
If you feel more relaxed moving or walking about then do so. Alternatively, sit comfortably, whatever you feel best doing.

No food or drink
Do not eat, drink, smoke or chew gum. They will all be heard by the caller and may even by magnified by the powers of modern technology. Treat the call as a formal interview in this regard.

Listen
Allow the caller to set the agenda and do most of the talking. Do not interrupt and wait until asked a question.

Converse
A skilled interviewer should be able to elicit detailed answers however, do avoid any yes or no replies. This is a two way conversation, so give detailed factual and honest answers and ask intelligent relevant and timely questions.

3Cs
Remember that the caller is interested in Capability, are you able to do the job, Commitment, are you willing to do the job and Cultural fit, will you fit with the organisation, the team and your boss.

Get an appointment:
The key target for you is to get an actual meeting with the organisation. Try not to leave this to the end of the conversation or it may be too late. Try to suggest a personal meeting as early as possible in the call.

Ask questions
It is vitally important that you ask questions and these will be the same as if it were a face to face interview. See Chapter 13 for questions you can ask.

Take Notes
Take notes, jot down the interviewers' name, position and any other relevant details. Notes will help if you are called to a face to face interview as you will have a better recollection of what was discussed, any questions you asked and the replies given.

A word of warning; some companies provide a telephone number and ask you to phone for an application form. These calls are often used to screen candidates so remember to treat this as part of the interview process too and be prepared to answer questions about your experience, achievements and why you are applying for the job.

Assessment Centres

When an organisation is recruiting large volumes such as in call centres and customer services it is becoming increasingly common to ask candidates to complete some form of pre-interview test or procedure. The main reason to do this is to answer two of the three questions primarily Capability, are you able to do the job and to a lesser extent Cultural Fit. You may be invited to attend an Assessment Centre where you take part in a variety of exercises or complete Psychometric Tests. The results of the tests and exercises will then determine if you are asked to a formal face to face interview.

Assessment Centres are usually run by external companies who specialise in screening out unsuitable candidates. Representatives from the recruiting organisation will have pre-set criteria based on the requirements of the role including skills required, qualifications, experience and personal attributes and they will work with the assessment centre to design a series of activities to find out if each candidate can meet this criteria.

A visit to the centre could well last a whole day and usually you are not given very much prior knowledge of exactly what is going to happen. This is designed to test your ability to work under stress and deal with unexpected eventualities.

Activities you may be asked to participate in include:

Role Play
A popular activity is to role play a scenario that occurs frequently in the job you are applying for. For example if it is sales role, you may be asked to persuade a prospective new client to purchase the company's products. If the job was as a supplier manager you may be told to pretend that the supplier is interested in increasing their fees and you have to negotiate or cancel the contract. In these situations the person you will be role playing with may be an actor employed by the assessment centre and their brief is often to take their cue from you. So if you get angry they will also, if you remain rational and calm and approachable then they will react similarly.

In Tray Exercise
Typically this will involve you being given an in tray and asked to complete all the activities contained within. This is a test of your skills in delegating, organising, prioritising and time management. Be aware, you will probably not have enough time to complete all the tasks and you may be interrupted by a phone call as part of the exercise. This is designed to test your adaptability under stress.

Case Study

Either as part of the in tray exercise or as a stand alone you may have a case study to complete within a limited time which may involve some number crunching or use of other technical data. Again this is a test of your skills under pressure and quite often there is neither a right nor wrong answer however you will be expected to argue the reasons for your decisions competently.

Practical Exercise

This can take place outside or inside, as part of a team or as a sole effort. The exercise could take the form of an 'outward bound' activity which involves completing a task such as getting a team across a river with limited equipment and under time constraints. Once again this is a test of team working, communication and analysis rather than of physical ability.

Simulation

Similar to a case study you may be asked to partake in a simulated exercise but one which is also closely related to something which may you may come across in the actual job. This could be dealing with a customer complaint over the phone for example.

Technical Tests/ Interview

Very common when applying for jobs in IT or where other specialised technical skill is required.

Physical Exercises

Candidates for customer services and call centre jobs are unlikely to be asked to take part in physical exercises and are more appropriate for applicants for the armed forces for example.

Other

Other typical exercises may include making a presentation. Typically you would not have any information given in advance and would be given instructions at the Assessment Centre with a limited time to prepare.

Group Discussion

A very common exercise and one which can be difficult for many candidates is a group discussion. You may be required to take part in a group discussion in which you and the other candidates are asked to discuss some topic or solve a fictitious problem. You would be asked to split into teams and report back and present your findings and solutions. You will be watched by external assessors and possibly by representatives from the recruiting organisation. They will be keen to see how you react within a group environment and to see if you a leader, a shaper, a finisher etc. Skills they will be making particular note of are interpersonal, communication, influencing, leadership, team working and negotiation. They will record your contributions so you must say and contribute something at some point during the exercise.

Tips on how to impress in group discussions

Be yourself: For example don't try to lead if that is not your natural tendency. You will either be found out at a later stage or if you are successful you may find yourself in a job for which you are not suited.

Listen: A key factor the assessors will note is how well you have listened and understood the instructions. If given verbally, make notes especially in relation to time restrictions. If paper based, re-read to make sure that you understand perfectly.

Contribute: You must contribute despite the fact that you may be nervous or unsure of the situation or the people surrounding you. Otherwise the assessors will not notice you.

Co-operate: If this is a team exercise, you must be seen to be a team player and over competitiveness or aggressiveness may not always be appropriate. Judge the situation based on the job being applied for.

Psychometric Tests

Tests to assess candidates for a role come in many shapes and forms and the choice of test depends on what the organisation is looking for in the individual. These are designed to assess each candidate in a reliable and standard manner and help overcome any bias which may be present in an interview situation. They are used either for screening purposes or as a complementary tool in addition to an interview.

Psychometric tests are the most common and include mental fitness tests, personality and behaviour type analysis along with interest inventories. Additionally, you may come across technical competence tests especially if the role is IT based.

All candidates receive the same test papers and these are administered in a controlled environment much like a school or university exam. Usually they will be paper based but increasingly can be computer based and are generally in the form of multiple choice questions. For personality and behaviour tests where there is no right or wrong answer we recommend answering as honestly as possible. For cognitive and mental fitness tests, which may be used to test ability or aptitude there will be one right answer. For these it is possible to practice in advance and there are many guides in publication both in print and on the internet. We recommend that you practice prior to the actual test to familiarise yourself with the types and formats of the questions

Treat Psychometric Tests as you would any exam. Give each question an allotted time and move on to next question when the time elapses.

Allow yourself about 10-15 minutes at the end to revisit any questions you left blank and make an attempt to answer them.

Dealing with Inexperienced Interviewers

We are often asked how to deal with inexperienced interviewers. It is a fact that many people conducting interviews may not have had any formal training in interviewing. You may find that you are more mature, wiser and more experienced than them. They may be newly promoted and while good at their job, interviewing may not be one of their skills. Irrespective, they will still be looking for answers to the 3Cs and while they may not be skilled in formatting questions correctly, you can go a long way towards making the interview experience a fruitful one for them. Offer information which is relevant even though the interviewer has not asked. They may have forgotten or lack the skill in proper questioning. If they ask you a direct yes or no type question, answer appropriately but add some key information which will help them make their decision. For example if they asked, "Did you enjoy your last job?" you could answer, "Yes, because it offered me some great opportunities to develop as a supervisor/manager and gain some excellent skills which I know I can use to contribute to this role"

An inexperienced interviewer may ask a closed question, that is, one with a yes or no answer. Be wary of answering just with a yes or no as you will come across as being uncooperative. Use this situation to add some key information which you know will help convince them that you satisfy the 3Cs of Capability, Commitment and Cultural Fit and can do the job better than anyone else.

Second Interviews

If successful during the first round of interviews you may be called to a second interview. There is very little difference in terms of interview structure or the types of questions you will be asked. If possible try to find out also how many people are being called back. Some companies re-call no more than 2 or 3 candidates and at this stage the choice is made largely on commitment, fit and personality as it is clear that all are well able to do the job. Our advice to candidates is to be yourself (within reason), as you will ideally want to fit with a boss and team to which your personality is suited.

Structured Interviews

You may come across something Structured Interviews and this is a version of interviewing whereby the interviewer has a script from which they are not allowed to deviate. An observer may be present in the interview room and they will note the answers being given and will look for key words. This format is used in an effort to make the interview process as standard and as fair as possible and is being adopted increasingly in large organisations where many managers are interviewing for the same type of position at the same time. Studies have shown this technique to be about 5 times more accurate than traditional interviewing in assessing and choosing the right applicant.

Chapter 4

Secrets of Successful Interviews

Proper Preparation

A common mistake made by many interview candidates is thinking that they can just arrive at the interview and 'wing it'. This works for some however for most a successful outcome is rare. With just a couple of questions it becomes very clear whether the candidate has spent time preparing or not. For example, they may have no idea of the company, it's products or culture and this begs the question why they want to work there at all. Our experience and that of our associates who have been interviewing for many years is that the key to successful interviewing is proper preparation. Whether you are invited for an 'informal' chat or a formal presentation in front of the Board of Directors it is essential that you prepare and practice as much as the time frame will allow.

With proper preparation you will be able to anticipate the questions you may be asked and prepare and practice your answers in advance. You will know what the organisation's needs are and will be able to match your skills exactly and convince the interviewer that you are the right person for the job. You will discover what key competencies are required for the role and can match your achievements to these. Having the right clothes, bringing the correct items, knowing where the interview is being held will all go towards helping you make a great first impression and in the process reduce and eliminate any nervousness you may feel. It is also during this preparation phase that you can take a moment and ask yourself why you are going to this interview and what you want to get from it. It may be that this is the job you have been waiting your whole life for or you may not be completely sure if it is right for you but want to use it as an information gathering exercise and to learn more about the company and its way of working. Irrespective of your motive we recommend that you approach each interview as if it was for your dream job and prepare extensively.

 Be wary of doing interviews just to get practice. It is often recommended that you attend a few interviews for jobs you are not interested in. While on the surface this seems like a good idea you may find that the interviewer will pick up on your lack of interest and you will not get the job. You need to consider the impact one or more rejections can have on your confidence. We would suggest that a mock interview with a colleague or partner is more effective.

Confirmation

Most likely you will have been invited to interview by letter which should include the interview date, time, location, name of interviewee and will ask for confirmation that you can attend. First thing to do is to ensure that you can make the interview. Check you diary and if you have a conflicting appointment which cannot be changed then inform the interviewing organisation or agency immediately and request an alternative date. Most recruiters are fine with this provided it is communicated as early as possible

Find out what format the interview is going to take. Is it a meeting with one or more people, is it with the HR department or the individual you will be working for, is it in an assessment centre, is a presentation required, will there be a psychometric test. If this information is not given a simple phone call to the HR department of the recruiting organisation or the secretary/personal assistant of the interviewer will generate this detail.

If the job is being recruited through an agency then they will have a duty to ensure that you are as prepared as possible and should obtain this information for you. We will take you through all of the above interview scenarios in the next section but it is vital that you know as much as possible about the interview before you actually get there

Research the Company

Researching the interviewing organisation is essential for three reasons.

1.	Through this process you will discover just what the company does, how strong is the company financially and does it have a bright future. By demonstrating your knowledge during the interview you will give an impression of interest, keenness and enthusiasm which is highly regarded by interviewers.

2.	You will have additional information to analyse just what the company is looking for, what do they need now or in the future. You will be in a strong position to match your skills to the company's requirements, you can better anticipate likely questions and can focus your answers during the interview to sell yourself.

3.	Most importantly you can go some way to discovering if the company is right for you, does its culture and values match those of yours, do you believe in the integrity of its products.

How to Research

Use the Web
Most of us have access to the internet and this is a great source of free information. Most organisations will have a web site which will give details of their products, locations and you may get some clues about the culture from photographs and phrases used.

Many research sites give free information although some of this will be subscription based. For all publicly quoted companies any of the share dealing sites will have this information available and forums on share dealing sites will give an insight into the company's current and anticipated performance.

Sales Brochures
A phone call to the sales department should elicit sales and marketing material from the company and this of course would be free. These can reveal information about products, sales trends, past performance and future plans such as expansion to new offices or the launch of new products.

Annual Reports

If you want to delve into the financial detail then you will need the latest published accounts. They provide historic information usually and while somewhat out of date will give a good overall view of where the company is coming from.

Ask your friends

You may know someone who worked or is working for the company. They will be your most valuable source of information on culture and values.

As interviewers, we are always impressed when an interviewee is able to show some knowledge about the company and its products or plans. It says that they are intelligent, enthusiastic and likely to accept the job if offered. It certainly gives them an edge over someone who has done no obvious research at all.

Ask around. You may actually know someone who works or has worked for the company and may even know your prospective boss. It could help you decide if you want the job or not!

Carry Out a Trial Journey

Depending on the location of the organisation or company it may be possible to make a trial journey and visit the offices prior to the interview. This will help immensely with your preparation in practical and emotional ways and will contribute to your research.

You will be able to check the exact route to the offices and decide whether it is best by car or public transport. If you are going by car you can check if there are any likely hold ups, road works, and problem areas and can also find out about parking either provided by the company or nearby.

If by train or bus you can discover the scheduled service times, the duration, platforms and distance to the office from the train station or bus stop. In both cases allow yourself plenty of extra time to arrive at your interview.

During your trial journey, take the opportunity to visit the company's reception area and pick up any brochures or marketing material that is available.

Make a note of the people you see working in the offices. How are they dressed, how old are they, what is the atmosphere like, friendly or stuffy, and what are other visitors wearing. All of this will help give you clues as to the type of culture the company is adopting and will help you decide if you fit or not.

The worst sin in interviewing is to arrive late and excuses about traffic jams or train delays do nothing to help.

If at all possible complete a trial journey and visit the office or location some days prior to the interview. Not only will you learn about the journey duration and any problems you may encounter, you will feel more relaxed on the day of the interview. It will be so much more familiar.

Conduct a Mock Interview

It goes without saying that the most important element in any interview is your ability to communicate and sell yourself properly.

In Chapter 7 we show you how to predict the questions you may be asked and while knowing the questions and having some idea of the answers is essential, if you have not yet verbalised them you may find that they do not come across as you would like on the day. A simple and effective exercise to overcome this is to carry out a mock interview. This can be very powerful especially if you have not had an interview for some time or are changing careers into a new industry or job.

Follow these steps to carry out a mock interview:

Step 1
Use a script as included in Appendix I or create a script using the list of questions. Select a number of questions you would like to be asked and do include the ones you fear most!

Step 2
Find a willing partner who will act as the interviewer. This can be anyone you know, a colleague, partner, friend, however they must act the part as real as possible. You can have more than one person if you want to create a panel type interview scenario.

Step 3
Give the script, job description or advertisement, your CV/Resume and the covering letter if you have one to your interviewing partner.

Step 4
Create an office type environment or use an actual office if available. Many interviewers will still sit behind a desk however increasingly interviews now take place without a desk or table in between the interviewer and candidate.

Step 5
In consultation with the 'interviewer' set a duration for the mock interview and we would suggest a time of 30-45 minutes.

Step 6
Begin the role play by knocking on the door and entering when asked to do so. To get the most from the exercise, both you and the 'interviewer' should act as if this was a real interview.

Step 7
During the interview your interviewing partner will make notes based on their impression of your answers. When the interview is over, ask for feedback in terms of how you first appeared, how convincingly did you answer your questions, what was their overall impression, how could you have improved, what would have worked better. Similarly, give feedback in terms of how you felt, what you wanted to say but may not have communicated properly.

Step 8
Review your answers and then repeat the process with your interviewing partner. You will find that you are more relaxed, much smoother in giving your answers and create a more powerful impression second time around.

If you have a camcorder, why not use this to record your mock interview and then play it back later to see how you performed. This can be an excellent device allowing you to appraise your own performance in an objective way. Use this also if you don't have a partner available. Simply ask yourself the questions, give the answers directly to the camera and review your performance afterwards.

Chapter 5

On The Big Day

The Interview Structure

Most interviewers will adopt a pre-set interview type and style or number of styles that are either recommended by the organisation or a personal preference. The structure of the interview however is more standard and follows a set pattern which is as follows:

Introductions

This is the initial greeting and this 'small talk' is designed to make the candidate feel comfortable. It allows them to settle into the interview, place their coats and bags appropriately and sit in the chair. It is during this time that the interviewer will first formulate an impression. Taking cues from the candidates dress, body language and first words, many interviewers make up their minds within the first 30 seconds who to give the job to. It is for this reason that you must make a great first impression and later in this chapter we give you all the information you need to do so.

Setting the Scene

After introduction, the interviewer will set the scene and thank you for coming, reiterate the purpose of the interview, state how long it will take and possibly the goals of the interview. They may talk a little more about the organisation and job being recruited for and if this is part of a round robin interview they will advise you who you will be seeing next.

At this point your most powerful tool is your ability to listen and analyse. Is the interviewer giving any clues as to the format or style of the interview, are they giving more information about the competencies and requirements of the role which will help you to tailor your answers and guide you in the questions you need to ask.

Exploration

Exploration is all about the questions and answers and is a two way process designed to match wants and offers and answer the 3Cs. This is the time to show that you meet the 3Cs, that you are Capable of doing the job, you will be Committed and that you match the Cultural Fit of the organisation. During this phase you will also ask questions which will help determine if this job is right for you.

Selling

After the exploration stage MAY come the selling stage. If during the exploration stage the interviewer determines that you are a contender for the role they may choose to take this time to try to convince you that the role and the company is right for you. In other words they will do some 'selling'. This does not mean however that you are being offered the role; it simply means that they want to maintain your interest. Do not take this as a cue to negotiate or discuss salary or benefits. A tip for you at this stage is to indicate that you are very interested even if this is not the case. If offered the job, this will boost your confidence and you can always use it as a bargaining tool either in your current role or against other offers.

Closure

The last stage in the interview structure is closure. You will probably be about to breathe a sigh of relief that the interview is almost over however it is vital that you leave a strong lasting impression. In Chapter 13 we talk you through the key steps to make a great finish and keep your profile at the forefront of the interviewers mind when making their decision.

In terms of timing, exploration will take up most of the interview about 75% of the time. Introduction and setting the scene will take approximately 10% of the time, selling 10% and closure 5% although these can of course vary.

How to Dress For Success

An interview is more than just questions and answers and the interviewer will be making a decision based not just on the answers you give but on a whole range of non-verbal signals. Recent research has shown that in terms of our tendency to from impressions:

> 55% is based on appearance
> 38% on tone of voice
> 7% on the words being said

When this is coupled with the fact that a decision can be made in the first 2 minutes of a job interview and possibly in the first 30 seconds it goes without saying that what you wear has a huge impact. The right choice of clothing and accessories can make a very powerful first impression and win you the job or conversely wearing the wrong clothes can lose you the job.

This section focuses on how you look and what to wear or not to wear to a customer services or call centre job interview. Your visual image conveys a powerful message not only about how you feel about yourself but can give clues as to your attitude towards the interview itself. If you turn up in your casual clothes you are telling the interviewer that you are not particularly bothered about the interview or the job. Conversely by dressing appropriately and professionally, you are saying that you care, that you are keen and want the job and that you respect the interviewer and the interview process. In addition, correct dress will reinforce the message that you can do the job correctly and that you know what you are doing. It will help reassure the interviewer that you understand the company's image and can be trusted to communicate it appropriately.

 As memory is based in visual images, quite often the interviewer will remember a candidate by the clothes they wear and when assessing and considering who to call for second interviews or who to offer a position to, proper dress will go a long way toward assuring the interviewer that you are that correct person.

Knowing that you are dressed right for the interview will add greatly to your feelings of confidence and self esteem and will help with any nervousness you may feel on the day. By following the guidelines on the following pages you can be sure that your entrance into the interview room will be effective.

General Guidelines

While many organisations encourage employees to 'dress down' maybe for one day per week and call centres often adopt a casual dress code, we would still recommend that you 'dress up' for the interview. Even if you appear a little overdressed it will show the interviewer that you have made an effort, are keen and respect the interview process. Dressing appropriately for a customer service job interview with most organizations generally means dressing conservatively and the following guidelines apply for both men and women:

- Use your research of the company to get an idea of the dress code. If you have made a trial journey you can see how the receptionists and employees dress. Even if the dress code appears to be casual we would still recommend that you err on the side of caution and dress up for the interview
- Dress conservatively and avoid bright, gaudy colours
- Smart business suits for men and women in navy blue or shades of grey are usually best
- Make sure that you feel comfortable in your clothing. If you have bought a new suit for the interview, wear it a few times beforehand so that you get used to it and it does not feel awkward
- Clean and press all of your interview clothing and polish your shoes
- Keep jewellery and accessories to a minimum. Avoid jewellery that jangles or swings when you move as this will cause a distraction. It may also provide you with something to fiddle with subconsciously during the interview which will give the impression that you are nervous
- If you normally wear facial jewellery (e.g., in your nose, tongue or eyebrows), remove all of it before the interview
- Clean and trim your fingernails
- Keep hairstyles modern and tidy and overall practice good hygiene
- Avoid fragrances, both perfume and aftershave. The choice of fragrance is a matter of personal preference and your interviewer might dislike your choice
- Use a briefcase or attaché to carry your paperwork. Take the interview invite, your checklist, 2-3 copies of your resume, reference letters, a sample of your work but only to be shown if invited to do so by the interviewer. Also have a pad and pen, which you can use to jot down your thoughts and key information as soon as the interview finishes. DO NOT bring a plastic bag, rucksack or any other superfluous baggage

 If the interviewer has made an effort to dress appropriately they will expect the candidate to be at least as well dressed if not slightly better. A candidate who turns up poorly presented immediately starts from a negative position. Use your research or trial journey to the company to get an impression of how other staff members dress and dress a couple of notches up from this. If in doubt however a conservative, professional look rarely goes wrong.

Job Interview Dress Guide for Women

Women's Suits

Women generally tend to have more flexibility when it comes to business dress and choices for an interview. A business suit does not necessarily have to be a dark two piece with a white blouse and sensible shoes. There is a whole range of outfits currently available which are fashionable, conservative enough for interview and can still look great in many other situations.

There may be almost too much choice so our advice is, if in doubt go with a conservative business look. This would include a business two piece suit with skirt or trouser combination. Colours can include shades of grey, from dark to light including charcoal, black and navy blue along with more modern colours such as dark browns, rust or greens.

Jackets should be well tailored and stylish and should flatter your build. Keep the look crisp and clean and avoid too much detail as this will detract from you and what you have to say in the interview.

A trouser suit is very modern and can prove to be a more individual choice than a skirt suit.

If you choose a skirt, ensure that the length is in keeping with current fashion and conservative tastes. You may not know your interviewer, how old they are, what their tastes are, etc, so it is best to stick with conservative business guidelines. Use your knowledge of the organisation and of the type of company when making your choice of suit. For example a pinstripe suite may give the message that you are ultra-conservative and might work great if you are interviewing for a position in law or investment banking but may but work for a job in television or media. This is where a trial journey to the company may help greatly with your choice of outfit.

Avoid wearing denim jackets or jeans, combats, hoodies and tracksuits of any sort.

Blouses/Shirts

Long sleeves are the norm here and avoid anything sleeveless even if you are wearing a jacket. Natural fabrics work best and you have a wide choice when it comes to colours. Plain colours such as white or cream can look great with darker business suits however you can also use colour to soften a conservative look.

Pattern can similarly be used to lighten a conservative look however avoid gaudy or flashy styles as they may cheapen your outfit.

You can wear a collar which always works well if interviewing for a bank or similar conservative organisation. Similarly a crisp white shirt without a collar can look great for a softer look.

Other

Choose shoes which complement the overall outfit. Darker colours work great with dark conservative suits and choose heel heights which reflect current fashions.

Avoid trainers, flip-flops, or over glamorous evening shoes however open toes or heels can work well depending on the type of organisation recruiting.

For stockings or tights neutral skin tones are best and do bring an extra pair in your handbag in case of laddering.

In terms of jewellery keep it to a minimum. A necklace, earrings and engagement or wedding rings are all fine. A ring on every finger is not a great look for interviews and large jangling earrings may cause a distraction.

While fashionable it is best to avoid fingernail designs and bright or gaudy coloured nail polish. Clear or no nail polish is best. Apply makeup sparingly and avoid unusual or bright colours.

While a handbag or purse is undoubtedly useful we recommend carrying a briefcase or portfolio into an interview instead. This will present a much more professional image and give the message that you are serious about the interview. Choose one that is smart, made from leather and either in black or dark brown.

Job Interview Dress Guide for Men

Men's Suits
Despite changes in fashions it is still best practice to wear a conservative business suit to a job interview. The best colours are navy, charcoal and light grey. Black is not recommended as it can appear too funereal and dull and pinstripes would be too formal for unless the role was in a banking or legal environment.

It is often thought that dark colours such as navy and dark grey give the wearer an air of authority and importance and for this reason we would not recommend light coloured suits such as beige or tan for a job interview. Either way, try to ensure the suit matches your colouring. Dark haired people generally look good in dark grey or navy while a lighter grey may look better on those with reddish or blond hair.

Shirts

Shirt colours vary greatly but our recommendation is to wear light coloured shirts in pale blue, cream or beige. While not at the forefront of fashion white is still very acceptable in interviews and can convey honesty and integrity. Shirts can be plain or with some form of stripe. Avoid dark shirts even if they are very fashionable or expensive as they will draw colour from your face and make you look nervous and possibly ill.

Always wear long sleeves even if your interview is in the middle of August. We particularly like double cuff sleeves but if you choose these do wear proper cuff links as opposed to the manufacturers cloth ones which come as standard with the shirt. A standard cuff is equally acceptable however avoid wearing wear cuff links with these, simply button as normal.

Ties

A key tip is to buy a normal priced suit but splash out on a good quality shirt and tie. This will make all the difference and can lift an ordinary outfit, make it look great and help make a powerful first impression.

Choose either a pure silk tie or a silk mix which are usually wrinkle free and easy to knot.

The colour should complement the suit and shirt and all should work together with your own colouring. Go with the conservative side of current fashion and avoid ties with cartoons, gaudy or loud colours, large dots or other outlandish patterns.

When knotted the tie should extend to just above the trouser belt with a large knot as per current fashion.

Other

Shoes should be low-heeled and conservative in a colour that matches your suit. Black or dark brown is best and try to avoid wearing light tan shoes, trainers, cowboy boots or other casual footwear. A tip is to polish your shoes before the interview. You may have very expensive, dark shoes but if they look scruffy or dull they will detract from the whole image and may spoil all your good work.

Shoes can be laced or loafer in style, both are acceptable.

Socks should also be dark in colour and should complement your suit. If in doubt go with plain black and avoid any garish colours or patterns. Make sure they are long enough so that when sitting down your bare leg is not visible.

Wear an overcoat or raincoat to the interview if necessary, however take it off as soon as you reach the reception area and if possible leave it outside the interview room.

Make sure all other accessories are good quality and complement the outfit and the image you are portraying. Avoid cheap, cartoon watches and do not wear any excessive jewellery, pins or religious medals.

Belts are essential and should match your suit colour. Choose good quality leather belts with a small metal buckle, one that does not detract attention from the rest of the outfit.

Do not wear chains or other jewellery that is visible bar a wedding ring.

Overcome Interview Nerves

Introduction

The first and most important thing to say on the subject of interview nerves is that EVERYONE experiences them. As with public speaking there are very few people who are able to stand up and speak in front of a roomful of strangers and not feel some degree of nervousness. Top actors, television presenters, senior businessmen all succumb to nerves and all have their own way of coping and getting on with the job.

 It is the same in the lead up to and during a job interview. It is an unfamiliar and artificial setting made all the worse if you don't know what to expect. It is very much based in our fear of the unknown and while some people can control their nerves others feel trapped and are unable to perform at their best. Indeed we have seen scenarios where a good candidate has panicked and as a result has performed poorly at the interview and missed out on the job offer.

In this section we will give you some great tips and techniques to help you overcome and reduce your interview nerves allowing you to communicate and sell yourself effectively. Notice that we say reduce because in our opinion it is neither possible nor desirable to eliminate nervousness completely. A candidate who arrives at an interview feeling normal levels of nervousness will come across as energetic, enthusiastic and keen to take on the role. On the other hand one who arrives and does not show any of the above could be seen to be bored, not interested and ultimately is unlikely to be offered the job.

Why do we feel nervous?

Our feelings of nervousness are a natural reaction to unfamiliar situations and are based on the 'the fight or flight response'. This is a very fundamental part of our make-up and forms a highly efficient survival response used by our ancestors when confronted with potentially dangerous situations.

While a job interview would hardly be classed as a dangerous situation, it is an unfamiliar one and one where we need to be on guard and give the 'right' answers. As we start to feel nervous or anxious, many changes start to happen in the body almost all of them subconsciously. In response to the release of hormones such as adrenaline, your blood pressure increases and breathing speeds up preparing you for muscular effort, i.e. the fight or flight. For most people that is as far as it goes and they feel energised and ready. For others this can be more intense and they may experience some shakiness, muscles may be tense, the palms of the hands and feet may become either sweaty or cold and clammy.

At the same time blood is moved away from the stomach to the major muscle groups and one can feel light headed or the need to go to the bathroom. The mouth may be dry and breathing may be laboured. We follow with six effective techniques all proven to help reduce nervousness.

Six Effective Techniques

1. Proper Preparation

Imagine going into a room you have never been to before, full of strangers none of whom you have never met. How nervous would you feel on a scale of 1 to 10 with 10 being highest? Now imagine going into your own living room full of your closest friends and family. How nervous would you feel in this scenario, probably 0 or maybe 1 if it was a party or special occasion. The key here is that one situation is familiar and the other is not and the degree of nervousness we feel is directly related to how much prior knowledge we have.

By following the guidelines in this book and by preparing properly for your job interview you will make an unfamiliar situation into a familiar one and in so doing will reduce your nervousness significantly. Put as many of the tips and techniques into practice as the timeframe will allow. Research the recruiting company, analyse the job description, visit the offices where the interview will be held, carry out a mock interview at home, make sure you have the right clothes and accessories to make a great first impression and ensure you have all the right tools and information ready for the big day. All of these will help you prepare mentally and help you feel that you are 'coming home' when you arrive at the interview.

Format your own answers for as many questions as possible. Practice and repeat until you can say them fluidly, smoothly and above all naturally. Use your own words and feel comfortable with what you are saying. You will not be asked all of these questions because there is not enough time but our experience shows that there is an 80% chance you will be asked some of the questions we have listed. Other questions will be specific to you and your achievements so you also need to be very familiar with your CV/Resume.

2. Arrive on Time

There is nothing worse for you as a candidate than having to rush to an interview. Your body will be in a physical state of flight and combined with the worry about being late, the potential embarrassment, the risk of missing out on the job, all can trigger an anxiety attack. Not a good idea and we suggest that you time your journey to arrive about 20-30 minutes early at the interviewing offices. Do not however report to reception until 10-15 minutes before the start time. You can use the free time to relax, breathe, study your CV/Resume, read a book or whatever you feel most comfortable doing.

3. Use Body Language

Smile and stand up straight with shoulders back. This will give your subconscious a message that all is ok, it is not a dangerous situation and there is no need to initiate the fight or flight response.

If you suffer from either sweaty or cold hands simply pop into the bathroom prior to the interview, wash your hands and dry. They should stay warm and dry until you have completed the necessary introductions and handshakes.

4. Positive Mental Messaging

Nervousness can sometimes be acerbated by the negative messages we have running around in our heads. Things such as 'I'm not really good enough for the job', 'I might freeze and won't know what to say' or 'If I don't get this job no-one else will want to hire me' etc. If you analysed these messages rationally none of them would be true however much they 'feel' true. Counteract them with positive messages such as 'I can do this job'. You know this because you would have been screened out long before the interview if you could not. Having practiced your answers you will of course know what to say and say it well. Tell yourself that this is not the only job for you and it is just one of probably thousands you could do, many of which might be better.

Don't try to compare yourself to the other candidates. You have no idea what they are like or what they are offering. Tell yourself you are the best person for the job because chances are that is the truth. You know what the job requires and you know what you can do. A useful technique is to create a mantra such as a phrase like 'I know I can do this job and I will give a great interview' and repeat it silently leading up to the interview. It is surprisingly how well this works and how it can overwrite the negative messages.

5. AWARE

This is a common technique taught by psychotherapists to clients suffering from anxiety and can be used to help with any nerve inducing situation.

A = Accept your nervousness. Remember it has a purpose and is useful to you.
W=Watch it. Try to observe it as if from a distance.
A= Act normally and use 7/11 breathing. Slowly and naturally breathe in to the count of 7, using you diaphragm to inhale deeply into your stomach. Exhale slowly while counting to 11.
R= Repeat the above steps about 5-10 times and you will notice your anxiety disappearing
E = Expect the best and use your positive mantra

6. Deep Breathing

- Place one hand just above your belt line, and the other on your chest, right over the breastbone.
- Open your mouth and sigh, as if someone had just told you something really annoying. As you do, let your shoulders and the muscles of your upper body relax down with the exhalation.
- Pause, for a few seconds.
- Close your mouth. Inhale SLOWLY through your nose by pushing your stomach out.
- Pause briefly for whatever time feels comfortable. However, be aware that when you breathe this way, you are taking larger breaths than you're used to.
- Open your mouth. Exhale through your mouth by pulling your stomach in.
- Pause.
- Repeat steps 4-7 and continue for a couple of minutes.

Both 5 and 6 can be practiced just before the interview without drawing any attention to yourself and can be very effective in helping you to relax.

Last Minute Check

By now you have confirmed your attendance at the interview, researched the company as extensively as time will allow, completed a trial journey and visited the company's offices. You may have had a mock interview and ideally practiced your answers extensively.

This action deals with a final checklist to ensure that you have everything in place before your interview. We would recommend that you go through this list on the morning of the day before your interview thus allowing you sufficient time to fill in any gaps.

We have created a template for you to use which you will find on the following page. By organising and sorting all the details relating to the interview beforehand you are left free to concentrate on the key objective which is to perform well, to sell yourself and to learn if the job is right for you.

Included is a list of information you should have to hand and items you should take with you to the interview which should include the address of the interview and contact telephone numbers. Take the interview invite, your checklist, 2-3 copies of your CV, reference letters, a sample of your work but only to be shown if invited to do so by the interviewer.

Also have a pad and pen, which you can use to jot down your thoughts and key information as soon as the interview finishes and if making a presentation take the relevant equipment such as a laptop or memory stick as well as hard copy back-ups in case of technical problems.

Interview Checklist

Interview Date:	
Interview Time:	
Job Being Recruited for:	
Organisation:	
Address:	
Location of Interview – (Office)	
Name of Interviewer(s):	
Title:	
Phone: (Reception)	
Phone: (Interviewer)	

To take with me:	3 copies of CV/Resume ☐
	Presentation material,
	   Laptop, ☐
	   Memory stick, ☐
	   Hard copy ☐
	Samples of work/reports ☐
	Checklist ☐

Key job competencies	
My key strengths	
Summary of Organisation (Products, Industry, Plans)	
Questions I will ask:	

Make a great first impression

First impressions really count and it is during the first few minutes of the interview that you can win or lose the job offer. Follow these guidelines relating to both verbal and non-verbal language to make a great first impression.

Smile and enter the interview room

We are all human and a smile has a very deep effect on those who give and receive it. Remember the interviewer may also be a little nervous and the message you will give to them with a smile is that they are liked and trusted and in an interview situation this immediately helps set a more relaxed environment. Smiling will not only show you to be a confident, open and friendly individual but it will instil in you a feeling of self confidence.

Shake Hands

In the Western World a handshake is an accepted form of introduction however be aware that in some cultures a handshake may not be common. For example in Japan a low bow is normal and in certain Muslim cultures it is not usual for women to shake hands. Follow the interviewers lead and give a firm and warm handshake if offered.

For some people nervousness can cause cold hands. A tip is to pop into the bathroom just before the interview and run your hands under the hot tap or dryer to warm them up.

Make Eye Contact

Again this is an important piece of body language which reassures and shows confidence.

Greeting

"Hello Mr/Mrs/Miss Jones, I am Samantha Smith, pleased to meet you"

Using 'small talk' to make a big impression

During the introduction stage there will usually be some small talk used as a form of ice breaker. This can be about the weather, health, travel etc.

Remember that this is all part of the interview and your answers can be used to create a very favourable first impression.

For example a typical question might be: How was your journey today?' or 'Did you find the offices ok?' This is a great opportunity for you to demonstrate the preparation you have made by answering 'My trip was great, I did a trial journey last week to check the route and it was very easy and pleasant' or 'I know the route very well, in fact I popped into reception last week to pick up some marketing material, I wanted to know more about the company and your products.'

This will show to the interviewer that you are:

a. Capable of taking the initiative
b. Committed and willing to take action
c. You have studied the company and more likely to think that you will Fit Culturally

Immediately and very subtly you are beginning to answer the 3Cs and the interviewer knows that if you are employed, travel will not be an obstacle.

 A word of warning, however, if your journey was awful or if you feel ill, do not say so. There is nothing worse than starting off the interview on a negative both for the interviewer and for you.

Watch your Body Language

During the introductions and throughout the interview it is best to remember the following do's and don'ts:

Do Not......
- Use first names unless asked to or try to act familiar or chummy with the interviewer
- Smoke, eat or chew gum
- Drink - while it is polite to accept a drink if offered and useful if you suffer from dry throat, make sure that there is somewhere to put it, like a desk or side table. A rattling cup and saucer is a dead give away and will show nervousness. If in doubt just say "No thank you, I just had one"
- Fiddle with paper, pen or jewellery

- Take notes, as this may result in fiddling with the above and you may look as though you are not listening or concentrating
- Read either from a script or from your CV/Resume. This will suggest that it is made up
- Sit down until invited to do so
- Argue with the interviewer
- Discuss controversial subjects
- Show reports, papers or any other samples of your previous work unless requested
- Look at your watch as this will indicate lack of interest and boredom

Do…..

- Remove your over coat and place either on a hook or spare chair
- Put your briefcase, handbag, dossier on a spare chair or ideally on the floor beside you but not on your lap
- Switch off your mobile phone, this is preferable to having a silent but vibrating alert if you receive messages
- Sit comfortably with hands gently folded in your lap or on top of your legs
- Make eye contact with the interviewer. If in a panel interview make eye contact with the person asking the question but address your answer to all
- Ask for clarification if you are unsure of the meaning of a question
- Remember your interviewer's name and use it during the interview
- Act natural and most importantly be yourself

Remember that you are being interviewed from the moment you enter the interview premises. This includes the car park, the reception and the staff canteen if there is one. Each person you meet can be asked for an opinion of you and this is especially relevant for the person who collects you and takes you to the interview room.

Arrive in reception about 10 minutes early for your interview but no more than 15 minutes. It can be off putting if a candidate arrives too early as the interviewer has to think about where to put them and is aware that they are waiting.

Chapter 6

Interview Questions Analysed

At a customer services and call centre job interview you can be asked questions in many shapes and forms and which can be phrased in a multitude of ways. Trying to learn all the various combinations is an impossible task, however, by remembering that the interviewer is interested in three factors, Capability, Commitment and Cultural Fit you will be able to answer any question thrown at you with ease. In this chapter we discuss the most common forms of interview questions that you will encounter.

Six types of interview questions

1.   Behavioural Interview Questions

Also called Situational, these are used as a tool to discover how your past performance in a previous role may contribute to the job being recruited for. The interviewer will ask open-ended questions relating to your behaviour in past or hypothetical situations and will try to match your answers to pre-set requirements of the role.

Behaviour based questions require you to provide specific examples and usually take the form of:

- Tell me about a time when you....
- Give an example of a stressful situation you found yourself in and what did you do.
- Describe a situation which caused you problems and how you resolved it.

A technique to use when answering behavioural questions is what we call **iPAR**:

I = Talk about the part you played in IDENTIFYING or noticing the problem
P = Describe the PROBLEM, situation or task
A = Talk about the ACTION you took
R = Describe the successful RESULT by using figures and data to illustrate the benefit to the company.

Always use "I" rather than "we".

2.   Competency Based Interview Questions

The word competency is widely used in business environments and refers to the skills that are necessary to achieve a good performance level in the job. Every job will have a set of key competencies, some of which are essential and others desired and all are required to do the job properly. In preparation the experienced interviewer will draw up a list of 3-4 questions relating to each competency and directed towards discovering if the candidate has the skills necessary for the job.

Examples of Competency Based Questions are:

- Tell me about a time you gave effective customer service?
- How would you respond if a customer called to complain?
- Tell me about a situation in your previous job where you used your communication skills effectively.

3.   Personality Based Interview Questions

These questions are designed to find out more about the candidate and help the interviewer decide if they will fit with the culture of the organisation. Bearing in mind that many direct personal questions such as, Are you married? and How old are you? are illegal, the interviewer will phrase the questions carefully such as 'Tell me more about you', 'How would you describe your personality?', 'What do you like to do outside of work?'

4.   Technical Interview Questions

This type of question will be direct and designed to find out your level of proficiency with a particular piece of equipment, software or system. If you have used a particular telephony system or customer management software you will be able to talk about this in detail.

5.   Stress Based Interview Questions

These are questions which put the candidate in an uncomfortable position and may be awkward to answer. They may focus on a potentially negative aspect of experience or difficult career period, for example, 'Why were you made redundant?', 'Why has it taken you so long to find a job?' and they will be designed to see how the candidate copes under pressure.

6.   CV and Resume Interview Questions

You will of course be asked questions specifically related to your achievements. The interviewer may choose to use a leading questioning style or a direct question and examples include:
'I see you worked at _____ Banks' Call Centre in _____, what was that like?'
'What were your main tasks as Team Leader at _____?'
'What is your greatest achievement?'
'Why did you leave _____?'

An interviewer will probably ask a combination of questions but the majority will be behavioural or competence based. Both types are designed to find out how well you will perform in the role with competence questions concentrating on your skills and training.

Common Questioning Styles

Every interviewer will have their own way of asking questions and this will depend on their level of experience. The most common styles you will come across are:

Open Questions: This is the most common type of questioning style and these usually begin with How, What, When, Why, Where and Tell me. These questions cannot be answered with a simple yes or no answer.

Closed Questions: These require a short specific answer and are used mostly for confirmation. They can be answered with a simple yes or no and if they are used frequently during the interview it may be that the interviewer is inexperienced.

Probing Questions: These will be used to follow up on a previous answer and are designed to elicit more detailed information. They will begin with "Tell me more about…" or "Just to clarify, what exactly…"

Leading Questions: These are questions which begin with 'I see you have managed a large team before?' or 'So you had a successful time with _____?'

Combination Questions: This is where the interviewer will combine two question into one statement and will use multiple styles such as 'What experience do you have in making presentations and how do you rate your skills in this area?

How to Give Winning Answers

During the exploration stage of the interview both the interviewer and the candidate will ask questions and partake in a dialogue. This is a two way process designed to match wants and offers and answer the 3Cs. This is the time for you to show that you meet the 3Cs, that you are Capable of doing the job, that you will be a Committed and that you match the Cultural Fit of the organisation. During this phase you will also ask questions which will help determine if this job is right for you.

- Listen to the question being asked. If you are unsure of the meaning or phraseology then ask for the question to be repeated or repeat the question back yourself. Say 'Can you please repeat the question, I'm not sure what you are asking?' or say 'Can I clarify what you are asking...'

- Answer the question that has been asked. Do not give an unrelated answer no matter how useful you think the information is.

- Don't waffle. Stay focused and give relevant, brief, concise answers. Avoid giving superfluous information.

- Be honest - Don't exaggerate or add on something which you did not do. You will probably be caught out and in the event that you are not and you get the job, you may find that you are unable to carry out some of your duties causing untold stress for yourself

- Answer in the first person. Use 'I' rather than 'We' even if the achievement was a team effort.

- Throw 'hooks' - For example, if you were involved in some great achievement and the interviewer has not yet asked about it, you can throw what we call a hook which is a statement at the end of an answer which is designed to whet the interviewer's appetite and encourage them to ask you to expand. You can then talk more about this particular achievement.

Dealing with Illegal Questions

In the UK and US a combination of the Race Relations Act, Sex Discrimination Act and other statutes forbid employers from discriminating against any person on the basis of sex, sexual orientation, age, race, disability, nationality or religion.

You should not be asked questions such as:

Are you married?
How old are you?
Where were you born?
How many children do you have?
Do you plan on having children?
Etc

Despite these laws you may find that an inexperienced interviewer could innocently ask the above in some form or other.

It is important that you do not get angry, upset or confrontational. Simply deal with the question honestly and naturally and then move on. Should the interviewer persist you could always say "I'm not sure of the relevance of that question to the role" but best not to make an issue out of it.

Chapter 7

How to Predict the Questions

For many people this may seem like an impossible task without resorting to a fortune teller. However, it is possible to predict the questions and our experience working with individual candidates shows that up to 80% of the questions that will be asked in the interview can be anticipated in one form or another. To do this we place ourselves in the interviewers' shoes and follow the process they go through when creating a job description and preparing for the interview.

- When writing the job description the recruiting manager will have listed all the key competencies, the essential skills required to do the job well. For customer service and call centre roles these will include good communication, excellent customer handling, decision making, team working, planning and organising, problem solving etc.

- In preparation for the interview the experienced interviewer will use the job description to help formulate the questions. For each key competency they will list 3-4 questions designed to draw out the candidate and discover if they can actually do the job.

- The interviewer may also have created or been given a person specification as part of the job description. This is a profile of the type of person who is likely to perform well in the role and characteristics such as confidence, focused, self-motivated, enthusiastic, reliable etc may be desirable. The interviewer will ask direct or indirect questions to test whether the candidate possesses these traits or alternatively they will listen for clues given in answers to other questions.

- We know that the interviewer is only interested in three pieces of information, the 3C's we talked about earlier. ALL questions will be designed to elicit answers to the questions, can you do the job (capability), will you stay and do the job (commitment) and will you fit with the company and the team (cultural fit).

In reality there are a limited number of questions that can be asked during a single interview and using these key pieces of information and following the step by step process on the following page you can create a list of questions which you are likely to encounter.

To do the exercise you will need:

1. Your CV or Resume
2. The job description and/or advertisement and
3. The person specification if one is available.

You can obtain 2 and 3 from the Human Resources or Personnel department or from the recruitment agency if one is involved.

Step 1: Read and analyse the job description or advertisement in depth and write down all the key competencies. These are the skills required to do the job and you should generally find that there will be between 3 and 10 of these listed. Typical competencies include Team Working, Communication Skills, Leadership, Persuading, Selling etc.

Step 2: Prioritise the key competencies from A to D with A being the most essential and D being desirable.

Step 3: For each competency list up to 4 questions. Use the list of questions in this guide to help and do bear in mind that some will be directly related to achievements and tasks listed on your CV/Resume. Please note that an experienced interviewer is unlikely to ask a direct question such as 'Are you good with customers?" because you will of course say 'Yes'. They may phrase it negatively 'Tell me about a problem you had with a customer" or 'What aspects of customer services do you find difficult?"

Step 4: Note down all the key personal characteristics which are required both essential and desirable and list 3-4 questions for each. These could be confidence, tenacity, enthusiasm, disciplined, creative, flexible etc.

Step 5 You should now have a selection of key competencies, personal characteristics and 3-4 questions listed alongside each. When you are happy with your selection of questions, use the answers in this guide to help formulate your answers. Refer to your CV/Resume and do use your own words and phrases and practice them prior to the interview so that you come across smoothly and naturally.

You will find that even if an exact question is not asked you will have a sufficient stock of answers and phrases in your head which can be used. Provided you bear in mind that the interviewer is looking for an answer to capability, commitment or cultural fit then with a little practice you should be able to answer any question which crops up with ease.

Chapter 8

Common Interview Questions

In this chapter we consider ten of the most frequently asked questions that are likely to crop up in any Customer Services or Call Centre interview. Some may seem very straightforward and 'easy' to answer but all will have a deeper sub text.

For example the question 'What do you like/dislike most about your current job?' is such a normal conversational question that one might be tempted to be very honest and open. This is what the interviewer is banking on and they will pick up on your answer and explore in greater depth any indications of weaknesses or problems.

Our advice with all the questions is to pause a moment and think about what the interviewer is really asking. Ask yourself, whether the question relates to Capability, Commitment or Cultural Fit or a combination and use the information to help formulate an appropriate response.

As with all the questions, we suggest using the sample answers as a guide only. Rather than repeating them word for word, create and practice answers using your own words and phrases and you will come across much more naturally and confidently.

Questions

Q1: Tell me about yourself

Q2: Why do you want to leave your current job?

Q3: What are your key strengths?

Q4: What are your weaknesses?

Q5: What do you like/dislike most about your current job?

Q6: Why should we select you for this job, what will you bring to the role?

Q7: Where do you see yourself in five/ten year's time?

Q8: What do you know about our company?

Q9: Why are you interested in this role and what is it that attracted you?

Q10: What is your Salary?

Q1: Tell me about yourself

How to Answer

This question will often be asked towards the beginning of the interview and can be used by an interviewer to get a general impression of you and your skills. It may also be used in a situation where the interviewer has not had time to read your resume. What is required here is a short commercial about yourself, which could include your name, your personal profile, key strengths, your most recent experience, a key achievement and what you will contribute to the organisation. Be brief, concise, relevant and limit your answer to no longer than 90 seconds. Don't ramble or go into detail but ensure that there are lots of interesting 'hooks' which will encourage the interviewer to say 'That's interesting, tell me more about that'.

Winning Answer

Good morning, my name is Danielle Jones. I have worked in Customer Services for the past three years with _____ in _____. In my current role I deal with customer complaints relating to credit card payments and am happy to say that I consistently achieve my targets in terms of number of calls and percentage of satisfied customers. I enjoy working in Customer Services very much; I have excellent communication skills and am able to respond to customers sensitively, calmly and accurately. Going forward I will be working in a Customer Services role within the same industry and your organisation is one in which I believe I could settle down and make a real contribution.

Losing Answer

Hi, I'm _____. I was born in _____ and lived there until a few months ago. I'm divorced now and have two kids and it's a bit of a hassle sometimes taking care of them on my own. I know I would be good at this job and I really need to get working at something so hopefully you will give me a chance.

This answer suggests that the candidate is desperate and the fact that the individual is having difficulty coping in their private life would ring warning bells for the interviewer.

Q2: Why do you want to leave your current job?

How to Answer

We recommend the following as being valid reasons for changing jobs although there may be others:

- **Advancement** - The opportunities for growth and development were limited
- **Challenge -** You had outgrown your current role and are seeking a new challenge
- **Stability** - You are looking to develop a long term career and your previous job did not offer that
- **Location** - There may have been too much travel involved and you are now looking for something closer to home

Above all, make your reason for leaving a positive one and do not complain about any aspects of your previous company or boss. The interviewer will be looking at your motivation for moving and trying to assess how realistic it is. For example if your expectations on promotion, reward, challenges, growth, and excitement are unrealistic they may conclude that you are unlikely to be fulfilled in any role and will move jobs again within a short space of time.

Winning Answer

I have been in current job for over five years and because of the size of the company there are limited opportunities for me to grow and develop further. I am looking to move to a larger organisation where I can settle into a customer facing career and be continuously challenged and my research suggests that yours is one in which I could do that.

Losing Answer

Well, I worked there for over two years and frankly I was a bit bored and needed to do something new. I think my boss picked up on this as well as we had a few arguments over the last few months. I'm sure he will be glad that I have left and I'm really looking forward to trying out something new.

This answer might suggest an individual who is restless and who may not be capable of settling down easily. A poor relationship with a previous boss should never be disclosed in the interview.

Q3: What are your key strengths?

How to Answer

This is a great question which will allow you to match your skills to the key competencies of the job and convince the interviewer of your ability to do the job better than anyone else. Key to answering this question well is to use your analysis of the job description as described in Chapter 7: How to Predict the Questions along with any additional research of the organisation you have completed. Ask yourself, what are the key competencies of the role and what key skills does the company need then tailor your answer accordingly. For example in any Customer Services role the key skills required will include: Excellent Communication Skills, Ability to deal with people, Planning and Organising, Decision Making and Team Working. Choose no more than three of your skills which are key to the role and which are essential for this particular job. Give examples of achievements where you actually used these skills and demonstrate the successful outcome as a result. You can also add some personal traits which are required in the role and interviewers always like to hear about enthusiasm, loyalty, reliability, determination.

Winning Answer

For example, if applying for a Customer Services Advisor role a winning answer might be:

> *One of my key strengths is my ability to deal with customers in a professional and sensitive manner. This is something I demonstrated in my last job where I was able to process customer returns efficiently and quickly and this was commented on by my supervisor in my annual appraisal.*

You could then finish off by saying… 'Overall I am a dedicated and enthusiastic worker and take pride in doing a great job.'

Losing Answer

> *Well, my wife tells me that I am excellent at DIY and in fact I do enjoy this type of activity. If I didn't have to go to work every day I would probably just potter around mending things.*

Candidates do sometimes provide unusual answers and this one did not get the job. If you have a particular talent but the job does not ask for that then don't mention it.

Q4: What are your weaknesses?

_____

How to Answer

The interviewer is trying to see if you have a relevant weakness, if you are aware of it and whether you understand its potential impact on the role. Most of all, they will be trying to judge if it will stop you from doing the job effectively. This is also a stress based question as most people feel uncomfortable admitting weaknesses especially in an interview environment. When answering it is very important that you are not tempted to confess all. While your frankness may be refreshing it will not help you win the job offer and we suggest that you choose something innocuous and certainly not something related to a core requirement of the job. A good example of an answer would be to turn a particular weakness into a developmental action, something you are improving on and ideally you should put the weakness into a past context and talk about how you overcame it.

Winning Answer

A good general starter is to say that you do not believe you have any weaknesses which would prevent you from doing an excellent job. This could then be followed by, for example:

My computer skills were a little rusty however I am taking a course in Microsoft Excel and Word which is very rapidly getting me back up to speed and which I am really enjoying. I am now able to write advanced macros which I was never able to do before.

Or

When I started my previous job, my delegation skills were not as good as I would have liked. The company sent me on a full management course where I learned not only how to delegate but also how to manage and motivate large teams which helped me to gain a promotion to Team Leader responsible for 12 agents.

Losing Answer

Be aware of using the standard false positives such as:

I work too hard, I spend too much time in the office I never see my friends, or I'm so passionate about my work, I sometimes lose sight of life outside.

These are not convincing and may even suggest that the candidate is inefficient.

Q5: What do you like/dislike most about your current job?

How to Answer

There are surely aspects to any job which one doesn't like but you don't have to mention them in the interview. With this question we would advise that you avoid the negatives. Concentrate your answer on what you liked about the job and relate these activities to the key competencies of the job being recruited for.

If you are pressed to talk about dislikes, use the reasons for leaving, lack of advancement opportunities, stability and challenge as mentioned in question 2.

Winning Answer

There was really nothing I disliked about my previous job. I worked in a great team with an excellent boss and I contributed a lot over the time I was there. The only reason I am looking to leave is to find a position within a dynamic organisation where I can develop my management skills further working with larger teams.

Losing Answer

I did not like having to attend meetings very much. There seemed to be one every hour and frankly I very rarely had much to contribute. I think people arrange meetings just to pass the time.

This candidate made the common error of criticising the previous employer by suggesting inefficiency. They also came across as being a potentially difficult person to manage.

Q6: Why should we select you for this job, what will you bring to the role?

_____

How to Answer

The interviewer is looking for a positive answer to the 3C's Capability, Commitment and Cultural Fit. This is an opportunity for you to convince them that you believe that with your past achievements and skills you can do this job, demonstrate with examples of previous experiences that you will be a committed employee and indicate why you think you will fit.

Be confident, strong, determined and remember the interviewer is looking for reasons to hire you not the other way around. Refer to the job description and the specific requirements of the role and align your skills, experience and achievement to those.

Talk in terms of the contribution you will make and if you are moving from one industry or sector to another a good phrase to use is 'transferable skills' which are those abilities and characteristics commonly required by all Customer Services companies such as excellent communication, team working, getting the job done, results oriented and focused.

Winning Answer

My career lies in Customer Services. It's a role I have always enjoyed and one of my key strengths is my ability to communicate with customers, understand their needs and satisfy them without compromising the organisation. These and my people management skills helped me to win promotion to Assistant Customer Services Manager in my current company.

Losing Answer

I am an enthusiastic person, a quick learner and always willing to try out new things. I am very ambitious and am keen to move up the career ladder as quickly as possible.

A reasonable answer that showed energy and drive however there was a risk that the candidate viewed the job as a stepping stone to something else and would leave within a short space of time.

Q7: Where do you see yourself in five/ten year's time?

How to Answer

The interviewer is looking for someone who will be committed and stable and who will stay in the job for the foreseeable future, certainly for a minimum of two years. Talk about your short term plans at this stage and relate them to the job being recruited for indicating your desire to do this particular job well and to be seen as a team player and committed professional. Talk about how you want to use your skills and experience to perform well and contribute to the rest of the team and the organisation as a whole.

While you may have goals to become a manager, director or change careers etc, unless they are relevant to the current role it is best not to share them. Instead show your desire to grow your knowledge and develop your skills in the current role and should an opportunity for promotion come along then you would hope to be in a position to apply for it.

Winning Answer

I see my long term career working within Telesales and I would really like to settle down with your company. My goals are to be regarded as a valued member of the team and to use all my skills to contribute towards the company's growth and should internal opportunities become available then of course I would like to be in a position to consider them.

Losing Answer

Well five years is a long time away and I don't really plan that far ahead. The only plans I do have is to take a career break probably during next year and travel around Australia and Asia for about three months. I'm very excited about that and I just need to get some money together.

This candidate did not get the job offer as they clearly would not be committed for a sufficient period of time.

Q8: What do you know about our company?

How to Answer

This question is all about how committed you are to the interview process, to the role and to the recruiting company. The interviewer doesn't want to waste their time and knows that if you are genuinely interested you will have done at least some basic research.

The wrong answer here is 'nothing'. You may as well leave the interview room now. This will indicate that you are not very interested and may only be doing the interview for practice.

If you have done proper research you will be able to talk reasonably fluently and candidates for higher level positions will be expected to know more than those at entry level.

Winning Answer

This candidate had not spent any time doing the research but rather than try to bluff they gave quite a good answer.

I concentrated on looking at the job description and person specification and making sure that I had the all right skills to deliver in the role. I am aware that your company is involved in the mobile phone industry and I look forward to studying your products in greater depth.

You may get away with this on a first interview however if called to a second, make sure you can talk about the history of the company its products and plans and quote facts and figures as available.

Losing Answer

I don't really know what you do. The agency sent me down to the interview and they didn't give me any information at all, not even the directions.

This is very often the case however it is the candidates' responsibility to research and get the necessary information about the company and its products.

Q9: Why are you interested in this role and what is it that particularly attracted you?

_____

How to Answer

Positive reasons for applying could include the company's profile, reputation, employee policy, growth plans, the jobs' variety, pace, prospects and the quality of the staff. When answering it is important to show the interviewer what you have to offer rather than what you hope to get from the company. Talk about the research you have done which will show the interviewer that you are serious in your targeting of this particular organisation, rather than simply taking whatever comes along.

Once again, use this as an opportunity to align your skills to the key competencies of the role. If good communication is essential, mention that you want to use these skills in this particular company, industry or sector. While the salary or other benefits package may be attractive do not mention it as being a reason for applying. The recruiter is looking for someone who is going to stay with the job for a considerable period of time, usually at least 2 years and may worry about your willingness to move should another attractive offer come along within that period.

Winning Answer

My career is in Customer Services, it is something I enjoy immensely and I'm very attracted to this Customer Services Manager role as I believe it will give me an opportunity to utilise the skills I have built up over the past five years as well as being a very exciting challenge for me.

Or

I have always wanted to work with your organisation and was delighted when I saw this vacancy as I believe I have the right skills to bring something special to the role.

Losing Answer

I want to be a Senior Customer Services Manager and this is a good stepping stone for me to get there quickly.

This answer does not reassure the interviewer that the candidate intended staying with the job for a reasonable period of time.

Q10: What is your Salary?

How to Answer

You WILL be asked about your salary and benefits and your salary expectations at some stage during the interview process. It may be by the HR representative, by the recruiting manager or by both.

Our advice is to calculate a salary range prior to the interview but avoid disclosing this information during the interview. The longer you can keep this to yourself the more negotiating power you retain. Some suggestions for dealing with salary questions are:

1. Do not talk about salary specifics. Try to talk about total package including benefits. By talking about total package as opposed to basic salary you can blur the boundaries a little.

2. Do not lie. Many companies do check your previous salary and it will be very obvious from your records whether you have lied or not.

Winning Answer

This role is quite different from my current job and I am not sure that the salaries are comparable. I would prefer to fit within your salary scales and the market rates for this type of position and I don't envisage that salary will be an issue.

Or

I don't believe salary will be a problem but I would prefer to learn more about the position and its responsibilities before I discuss it in any depth.

If pushed then talk about your 'package' as a range and include items such as bonus, pension, car etc.

My current package is in the range of _____ to _____ and includes bonus, pension and health benefits.

You could then ask 'Can you tell me about your bonus scheme?'

Chapter 9

Competency and Behavioral Interview Questions

In this section we provide answers to Competency and Behavioural Based Questions which all relate to the candidates ability to do the job. Every role will have a set of key competencies which are the essential and desired skills required to do the job effectively. For each role there may be up to ten competencies required and in preparation the experienced interviewer will draw up a list of 3-4 questions relating to each competency and all directed towards discovering if you have those necessary skills for the job. Questioning style could be a combination of behavioural, open or probing and in this section we give answers to questions relating to the most common competencies you will find in Customer Services jobs today. These are:

9.1   Customer Handling
9.2   Communication
9.3   Planning and Organising
9.4   Team Working
9.5   Problem Solving
9.6   Decision Making
9.7   Persuading and Influencing

9.1 Customer Handling

Q11: Can you give an example of a time when you experienced good customer service and explain why it was good?

Q12: Tell me about a time when you gave effective customer service.

Q13: Describe the most difficult situation you encountered in customer services.

Q14: How would you respond if a customer called you to complain?

Q15: What characteristics are required in a good customer services advisor/call centre agent?

Q11: Can you give an example of a time when you experienced good customer service and explain why it was good?

How to Answer

To be able to give good customer service it is important that a candidate is able to differentiate between good and bad service. Having awareness of when they received different levels of service as a customer the job holder will then be in a much better position to offer great customer service themselves. The interviewer is looking for the candidate to demonstrate recognition and a clear understanding of what constitutes good customer service and to be able to articulate why it was good. Customer descriptions of a positive customer experience include:

- 'I felt as though the agent knew me and knew exactly what I wanted'
- 'I felt understood, I was listened to and made feel important'
- 'I was well taken care of from the moment I stepped into the bank'
- 'The whole process was easy and a nice experience'

Winning Answer

I had to call my bank to complain about a credit card transaction that went through twice by mistake. My phone call was answered really quickly by a pleasant man who very quickly identified me and called up my account details. He understood my worry that I might have to pay interest on this amount and he was able to resolve the problem within minutes. I thought the whole process was very quick and easy and this for me was good customer service.

Losing Answer

I had to call my local power company to change my address. I waited five minutes to get through after which the agent passed me onto someone else. I don't know if this is good or bad service but is the usual case when you have to call big companies.

Clearly poor customer service and the candidate failed to identify adequately that it was so.

Q12: Tell me about a time when you gave effective customer service

_____

How to Answer

Not only is the interviewer looking for a clear understanding of what constitutes good customer service they also want to see that you have been able to give it in a customer facing environment.

Choose an example from your past experience, maybe linked to an achievement on your CV or Resume and talk through in detail. Use the following structure:

- Describe the scenario
- Talk about what you did to help or service the customer
- Give details of the successful outcome and any positive feedback or results that ensued.

Winning Answer

For me effective customer service is all about understanding the customers needs and fulfilling them in a way that appears to the customer as seamless and effortless. This is something I do everyday by ensuring that the customers receive the products they expect within the time frame agreed. One situation I recall was _____

And then talk about a situation where you gave particularly good service.

Losing Answer

I recall one very happy customer to whom I gave a refund when she returned an item she didn't like. Normally we are only allowed to do exchanges but it was Christmas Eve and I decided to be generous.

While the customer was happy, this candidate did not receive a job offer as they deliberately flouted company policy on refunds.

Q13: Describe the most difficult situation you encountered in customer services.

How to Answer

The challenge with this question is that admitting to a difficulty could indicate that you had problems coping in the past and this may affect your performance in the future. The key here is not to admit to any weakness when answering.

Our suggestion is to avoid the negatives and talk about challenges you faced at some earlier part of your career in Customer Services and which you overcame. Demonstrate that you understand the difficulties which are involved and that you learned as a result of the experience.

Winning Answer

When I started working for _____ as a Customer Service Advisor I had a very irate customer complain directly to me about a problem with a lost cheque book. He was actually shouting at me and initially I was very shocked and taken aback. I managed however to keep my cool and listened, made sure he knew that I was listening and that I understood the problem. He calmed down a lot and I ordered him a new cheque book which he received the next day. For me, it was a great lesson about the importance of listening to the customer and allowing them space to talk.

Losing Answer

I had a difficult customer once who would not listen to what I had to say. They kept interrupting when I was trying to explain company policy and it took me a long time to get my point across.

This candidate did not show a clear understanding of good customer service. It appeared that their goal in this situation was simply to convey a message rather than take time to understand the customers' point of view.

Q14: How would you respond if a customer called you to complain?

How to Answer

This question relates to your ability to deal effectively with potentially difficult customer situations and ones where you may have an angry or irate person on the other end of the line. If you are being interviewed for a customer facing role this question or similar may come early on in the interview along with others which will be designed to assess your skills in this area. Key words to use when dealing with complaints are;

- listening,
- showing empathy
- understanding the customers needs
- referring to company policy
- fulfilling the customer requirements
- showing initiative
- following up on agreed actions

Winning Answer

Working in Customer Services, we often get customer complaint calls. I'm aware that the key is to understand the customer's position and feelings without necessarily agreeing with them. We have a strict pre-designed company policy which I always follow which involves listening, recording, assessing, discussing and agreeing an action with the customer. I'm pleased to say that in 99% of cases I find that I can resolve the situation to the customer's satisfaction without any manager intervention which is much higher than most of my colleagues.

Losing Answer

I don't like having to deal with customers who complain really. They are generally rude and I just pass them on to my manager to deal with.

We concluded that this candidate lacked the confidence to do their job effectively. While training was available the employer preferred to make the offer to a candidate with a stronger skills base than this one appeared to possess.

Q15: What characteristics are required in a good customer services advisor/call centre agent?

How to Answer

The key qualities required for anyone working in a customer facing role such as a Call Centre Agent or Customer Services Advisor include:

- Communication skills especially verbal
- Interpersonal and people skills
- Ability to listen and empathise
- An understanding and respect for customers
- Persuasion and Influencing skills
- Negotiation and selling

All of the above are key and your answer should show an understanding of the part each of those skills play in an interaction with a customer.

Winning Answer

Having worked in a financial services contact centre for the past four years I know that the skills required to provide good customer service include an ability to listen and understand the customer's position, to discuss and agree an action which is beneficial both to the customer and to the company and to make sure that action is carried out to the customers satisfaction.

Losing Answer

Customers really need someone who knows how to fix their problem.

Not always the case.

9.2 Communication

Q16: Tell me about a situation in your previous job where you used your communication skills effectively.

Q17: What experience do you have in making presentations and how do you rate your skills in this area?

Q18: In your current or a previous role what levels of management do/did you have to communicate with?

Q19: Do you prefer to communicate orally or by writing and explain why?

Q20: How would you rate your ability to communicate with senior management /colleagues/ customers/ subordinates?

Q16: Tell me about a situation in your previous job where you used your communication skills effectively.

_____

How to Answer

For most jobs good communication skills are essential. Whether as a team leader or as a junior staff member being able to get your point of view across is crucial to success. Non-verbal communication is important and is a subtle skill however the most common form used in the work environment is verbal which includes both oral and written. This behavioural style question is a test to see how importantly you view communication and how good you are at it.

Winning Answer

For me communication is key to ensuring the successful outcome of any task. I'm equally skilled with both written and oral communication and use both effectively on a daily basis in my current job. Listening to my customers, understanding their needs, being able to discuss and agree a satisfactory solution with them is all part of making their shopping experience a good one.

Losing Answer

I tend to communicate with the team only as required. I believe that tasks are best completed if each person is informed only of their own situation.

This may work in certain organisations and especially where confidentiality is essential. However, in most situations an open and inclusive communication strategy is accepted as being best.

Q17: What experience do you have in making presentations and how do you rate your skills in this area?

How to Answer

Being able to make a presentation is a skill required in many different jobs and at a variety of levels but in reality this questions is unlikely to be asked of entry level customer service candidates. For Team Leader and upwards making a presentation could be a common element of the job. For example you may have to inform your staff of a change in company policy or tell your colleagues about a team achievement.

If you have made presentations you will be able to talk competently about the process you undertake in preparing, the structure of the presentation, addressing each member of the audience, using body language to emphasise key points, allowing time for questions and the successful outcome.

If not, the answer below is an effective way of answering.

Winning Answer

I have talked through many reports in meetings with colleagues and my boss but I haven't yet had the opportunity to make a formal presentation. It is something I am looking forward to doing.

Losing Answer

You will either have experience of making presentations or not and it is best not to bluff.

Q18: In your current or previous role what levels of management do/did you have to communicate with?

How to Answer

Good communication is essential in all roles and organisations and this question is designed to determine the range of contact you had through the organisational structure. Do not exaggerate to try and impress the interviewer. It would be highly suspicious for example if a Customer Services Advisor had frequent contact with the Call Centre Manager.

When answering, give some information about the type, format and reason for the communication you had with each.

Winning Answer

I mostly communicate and have meetings with my boss the Telesales Team Leader, to discuss targets, performance and any training and development plans. I did attend a meeting with the Head of Operations recently where I was asked to talk on behalf of the team about the new telephone system and this I found very interesting and exciting.

Losing Answer

I really only communicated with my boss. He preferred to make any further upward communication himself.

To improve this answer the candidate could add:

One of the reasons I am leaving is because I feel I am being held back somewhat in this role and I want to take on new challenges including communicating to a wider audience including senior management.

Q19: Do you prefer to communicate verbally or by writing and explain why?

How to Answer

Both oral and written communication is equally valuable. To choose one over the other could show a weakness or a lack of experience in using the one not chosen.

We suggest a more diplomatic answer to this question.

Winning Answer

I don't have a preference and I use the most effective method of communication which is relevant to the situation. For example, when communication frequent or daily messages to the team I would use email as this ensures that everyone is informed simultaneously. For negotiations or where persuasion is required I will always use a face to face meeting and follow up with written confirmation of agreements.

Losing Answer

I prefer using emails for most communications. I find that it is quick and easy and I can keep track of what I have said and when.

True but we concluded that with this answer the candidate showed resistance to conduct face to face meetings suggesting a lack of interpersonal skills.

Q20: How would you rate you ability to communicate with senior management /colleagues/ customers/ subordinates.

_____

How to Answer

This question is seeking clues as to your ability to communicate at various levels. You will not be asked all of the above, for example if the role is customer facing you might only be asked about your ability to communicate with customers.

Communication skills are key is so many jobs that to rate lowly would effectively put you out of the running for the job. Be positive with your answer and have an example ready to back it up.

Winning Answer

> *I would rate my communication skills as excellent. In my last appraisal my manager commented on these and specifically my ability to deal with difficult customer complaints. This partly explains why I was asked to mentor and help train new Customer Service Advisors.*

Losing Answer

> *I get along and communicate well with everybody.*

This answer will lead to further exploration and deeper questioning.

9.3 Planning and Organising

Q21: How do you organise your time?

Q22: Imagine it is almost close of day and your boss gives you 5 urgent tasks to complete. What would you do?

Q23: Describe a time when you were unable to complete a task on time.

Q24: How do you plan and organise for long term tasks or projects?

Q25: Tell me about a situation where your planning skills let you down.

Q21: How do you organise your time?

How to Answer

This is a competency based question designed to find out how good you are at time management, prioritisation and organisation. The interviewer will want to see that you have a clear understanding of the importance of planning and the ability to use these fundamental skills on a daily basis.

Your answer should detail the tools you use to plan and organise and include some examples of how you have put these into practice with successful results.

Winning Answer

For me, proper time management is essential. I always plan my day and prioritise the activities some of which I class as urgent and others less important. I make sure that I complete each task within the time frame allotted.

Losing Answer

I don't really bother planning in too great a detail. I know in my head what needs to be done and by when and it works really well for me. I always deliver on time.

While this candidate may have been successful to date by just 'winging' it, there was nothing to be gained by boasting about this in the interview. It only showed the candidate to be reckless and unreliable.

Q22: Imagine it is almost close of day and your boss gives you 5 urgent tasks to complete. What would you do?

How to Answer

This is a multi layered question and is asking many different things all at once. How do you deal with stress? Do you ever get angry with your boss? How good are you at prioritising? How flexible are you?

This is a great question for you to answer and show that you are adaptable, enthusiastic, able to cope with any eventuality and professional in your manner at all time.

Winning Answer

> *This is a regular situation in my current role and one which I am very experienced and comfortable in dealing with. I understand that the job needs to be done as quickly and efficiently as possible so I will prioritise and complete each task methodically. I make sure that all jobs are completed before I leave the office and I check with my boss to see if there is anything else that needs to be completed.*

Losing Answer

> *I will complete a prioritisation exercise and those which are not urgent I will leave until the next morning and do first thing.*

By making assumptions on the importance of each task this candidate may mistakenly leave vital activities unfinished.

Q23: Describe a time when you were unable to complete a task on time.

How to Answer

Inherent in this question is an assumption that you were working under pressure and to strict deadlines. The key here is to show that you recognise the importance of finishing a job on time and show that you can cope with potentially tight timeframes in a stressful environment.

The question is also phrased in such a way that you are being invited to confess to a potential weakness, a missed deadline. In a career of any length you will probably have had just such a situation and we suggest you choose something reasonable innocuous from an early part in your career and turn in into a learning and development lesson.

Winning Answer

I do remember when I started working early on in my career in Telesales, my manager asked me to finish off the monthly sales summary sheets and gave me until the end of the day to do it. I tried to do it all myself and didn't actually finish until the following morning leaving only 30 minutes for distribution before the start of the meeting when they were to be discussed. It was a nerve wracking experience and I learned the importance of meeting deadlines and ensuring that my manager is informed of progress at every key step.

Losing Answer

I have never missed a deadline in my career.

This may be true and the candidate would need to expand on the answer and give examples of how and why in order to convince the interviewer.

Q24: How do you plan and organise for long term tasks or projects?

How to Answer

This is a question which could be asked when recruiting senior customer services or call centre managers and those expected to lead or be involved with major projects. You will probably only be asked this question if this is a key skill that is required in the role or if you have shown on your CV/Resume that you have completed this type of activity in the past.

The key here is to show that you are aware of the methods used in long term planning and are able to use them effectively. When answering talk through the steps you follow and then give an example of where this was successful, quantifying the result if possible.

Winning Answer

> *The starting point for me is to understand the goal or the end result that I am trying to achieve. I will work back and clearly document and plan for each stage of the work with clear and measurable milestones being allocated. I will then lay out the activities required to achieve each milestone. Where other people are involved I will make sure that they are part of the planning process and know what is required of them and by when. This has worked very well for me and I used it when I implemented a new telephone router exchange at _____.*

We then asked the candidate to elaborate and tell us more about this achievement.

Losing Answer

> *I tend to know fairly early on what is required to get the project or task done. I will create high level plans which I use to monitor progress but these are usually for my own use.*

We would have expected this candidate to show the involvement of other people and the communication of plans so that all are clear on the goals and targets.

Q25: Tell me about a situation where your planning skills let you down.

How to Answer

As with all negatively phrased questions you do not have to give a detailed answer. You can very easily say, 'I don't recall a time when that happened". The interviewer may choose to explore deeper or more than likely will move on.

Out tip with these questions is to finish strong and turn them to your advantage.

Winning Answer

I don't recall a time when that happened. I always plan thoroughly and envisage every eventuality. I'm glad to say this process hasn't let me down yet.

Losing Answer

It is very easy to be tempted into revealing a weakness with this type of question. Think carefully before answering.

9.4 Team Working

Q26: Describe your team working skills and give an example of when these worked well.

Q27: Are you a team player and what role do you generally play in group situations?

Q28: What types of people do you get along with best and worse?

Q29: Tell me why you will fit with the team.

Q30: What experience have you had working on a team?

Q26: Describe your team working skills and give an example of when these worked well.

How to Answer

Within a Customer Services environment most daily activities are carried out individually but targets are very often team based and key skills required for good team working include, listening respecting, helping, sharing, persuading supporting and participating.

You need to demonstrate your ability to use these skills effectively to create a sense of collective responsibility and understand that you are all focused on achieving a common goal whether it is increased sales, more satisfied customers or faster response times.

Think about situations where you have led or been part of a team either in a work situation or as a personal project. This is a common question and it will do you well to have prepared some examples in advance of the interview.

Winning Answer

I work well within teams and enjoy the challenge of achieving common goals. I know that key to achieving goals is having the whole team working in the same direction. In a recent project involving my local community sports club of which I am a member, I initially listened to get a clear idea of the other team member's views. I made sure I knew exactly what my role was and the activities I had to perform and I worked closely with them to ensure we delivered on time.

Losing Answer

I work well with other people although I have been told I am a very strong character. I generally get my own way in group situations.

Getting the job done in this candidates view, does not necessarily mean that it is done in the best way possible. There was a risk that this individual would be more interested in pursuing personal agendas and goals and could have upset colleagues in the process.

Q27: Are you a team player and what role do you generally play in group situations?

How to Answer

There are various models and tests to assess where an individuals' natural place is in a group and these can show a person to be a leader, finisher, starter, shaper, co-ordinator, specialist or implementer. We have the potential to be all of these but one or two will be dominant. For example one might be a combination of a shaper and a finisher, where they will be active when the group is forming or when the project is being defined and then will push to achieve an end result as quickly as possible. Typically these types will have less interest in the method or process being followed.

Think about the part you normally play in a team and when asked this type of question it is best to be true to yourself. If you really are a strong team leader or prefer to take an active back seat in teams then do say so. If you try to portray yourself as something you are not you may find that you end up in a job for which you are not suited and this will cause you unwanted stress in the long term.

Winning Answer

Yes I am very much a team player and my natural style in a team environment is to be pro-active and supportive. I enjoy working with different types of people and I can adapt easily to any group situation and I find that I am naturally keen to move the work along and get the job done.. This worked really well in my last job where I was part of the Customer Care team for premier clients. We achieved all our targets and this I believe was due to great teamwork.

Losing Answer

Working in teams is fine with me, I can adapt to most situations. I don't really mind what role I play, I'm happy to do whatever comes along really.

The candidate did not have or give a clear idea of how they fit in teams and it seemed that they do not have good experience of team work.

Q28: What types of people do you get along with best and worse?

How to Answer

With this question the interviewer is trying to assess whether you will fit with the organisation, the team and with your new manager.

It is really asking how you interact with other employees at different levels of the organisation such as management, colleagues and staff reporting to you. Your answer could address all three levels and use key words such as 'hard working, committed, results oriented, supportive, confident, reliable, fair' to describe those you get on best with. As to those you do not get on with, it is best to be diplomatic and give an open answer.

Bear in mind that the interviewer is likely to be you new boss so choose your words carefully. This could be seen as a 'trap' question and certain answers could effectively say that you would not get on with the interviewer/manager/team.

Winning Answer

Diplomacy would suggest that an open answer is best:

I find that I can get on with all types of people. I am very adaptable, I can work independently or under close supervision and I understand that priority lies with getting the job done.

Losing Answer

I don't really like managers who try to keep me on too tight a leash. I like to get on and do my own thing and I find that managers who are very controlling limit my ability to work effectively.

This was quite a good answer and the candidate came across as being very independent and determined. Unfortunately, the position being recruited for required someone who was going to participate in a large team and who could be relied upon to follow company procedures very closely and it was felt that this person would not do so.

Q29: Tell me why you will fit with the team.

How to Answer

This could be perceived as a difficult question to answer as you don't know the team yet. However, your research of the job and company will help you get a good idea of what types of skills are required in the team. Your answer will then show that you possess these skills and you can talk in terms of what you will bring to the team.

In addition, you need to demonstrate flexibility to fit in with any team and good words to use include working towards common goals, strong work ethic, supporting, sharing, participating, respect, being effective and committed.

Winning Answer

From my analysis of the job description I understand that you are looking for a Customer Support Agent, someone who has got strong communication and customer awareness skills and these are some of my particular strengths. In my current role I am part of a team of twelve and am seen to be supportive and committed towards achieving the teams and the organisations goals at all times. I enjoy working with different types of people and I know that with the experience and skills I have I will fit and make a real contribution to your team also.

Losing Answer

I'm really flexible with teams and have always found that I can fit in with most people. In my last job my boss was quite a hard person to work with but I always got on well enough by just getting on with things. Working in teams is fine with me, I can adapt to most situations.

While this may seems like a good answer the candidate did not give a clear idea of how they fit in teams or what they would bring to this particular team. They also criticised their old boss which is never a good idea in interviews.

Q30: What experience have you had working on a team?

How to Answer

This is a very straightforward question and one which requires a direct answer. Choose a couple of examples of when you were involved with teams either as a leader or member. Describe the situation and talk about the skills you acquired and the learning and development opportunities they presented.

Remember, team work is evident in all aspects of life and not just in the work environment.

Winning Answer

I have worked with teams both in and out of work. In my last job I was part of a 25 person team charged with changing the way customers applied for mortgages. It was a great experience and I learned a lot from the people around me including how to communicate and interact with individuals many of whom had differing views and opinions.

Losing Answer

I have experience of working on teams but am also capable of working on my own. My preference is to get on and do my job and sometimes I find that large teams can slow the process down.

A better option would have been to talk about the team working experience only in a positive light.

9.5 Problem Solving

Q31: Describe a difficult problem you had to deal with.

Q32: Working in Customer Services what types of problems do you resolve on a daily basis?

Q33: Tell me about a mistake or something you did wrong in your previous job.

Q31: Describe a difficult problem you had to deal with.

How to Answer

The interviewer is trying to get a view of what you regard as difficult and whether this will impact on your ability to do the job effectively. As you are asked 'to describe', this is exactly what you should do however it is best not to admit difficulty with problems which are likely to occur as part of the normal day to day responsibilities of the role being recruited for. Choose instead a one-off example from a previous role, one which is unlikely to re-occur and be sure to demonstrate clearly that you resolved the situation and learned from it.

Give as much detail as possible and use the iPAR structure as follows:

- Talk about the part you played in IDENTIFYING the problem
- Describe the PROBLEM, challenge or situation
- Describe what you did to resolve it, the ACTIONS you took
- Detail the successful RESULT and use figures to illustrate.

Winning Answer

I was only in the job for 3 months when I noticed that our late delivery times had increased by 25% and we were receiving over 100 complaints per week from unhappy customers. I investigated further, I spoke to the production team and to the distribution manager and to the delivery men. I found out that the vans were old and prone to frequent breakdowns and as we didn't have a maintenance contract this involved taking vans off road to a repair shop. To resolve the situation, I put a proper maintenance schedule in place, I invested in a contingency plan so that there was always a spare delivery truck available and as a result late deliveries were reduced to less than 1%, much less than the average market rate of 3%.

Losing Answer

Well, just after I started my boss asked me to check out why the complaints had increased. I went through all the statistics and spent many late evenings trying to find some clue but had to give up. I think I was just too new to the place.

This candidate did not show capability, initiative or problem solving ability.

Q32: Working in Customer Services what types of problems do you resolve on a daily basis?

How to Answer

The range and variety of queries and problems which customers can present is vast. Common issues include, late billing, being overcharged, late arrival of goods, incorrect order delivered, item not working etc.

The key point when answering this question is to clearly demonstrate that you are able to resolve the problems without having to escalate them to your supervisor. Show that you are able to use you initiative, take correct decisions while ensuring that you adhere to company policy at all times.

Winning Answer

In my current job I deal with a lot of customer calls relating to charges for late payment of credit card bills. I deal with the customer sympathetically explaining the reasons for the charge and how it has been calculated and find that once they understand this they are satisfied. Some request a cancellation of the payment however I cannot do this. We have a procedure to follow with these problems and I ensure that I adhere to this without exception.

Losing Answer

I get a lot of complaints from customers who have been overcharged on their monthly credit card statements. Some of these I resolve quite easily and others I will pass on to my supervisor to deal with.

It was not clear enough that this candidate was able to deal sufficiently well with normal day to day issues.

Q33: Tell me about a mistake or something you did wrong in your previous job.

_____

How to Answer

We are all human and during the course of a career, mistakes and errors of judgement will inevitably be made. When answering this type of 'negative' question you should use an example from the past rather than the present. Turn it into a development or learning exercise and by showing that as a result of the mistake you grew as an employee and as a person will help increase your chances of success.

A word of warning, if your mistake cost your previous employer significant amounts of money or resulted in an operational disaster, don't mention it.

Winning Answer

A good answer would be to use something innocuous for example:

> *In the first week working with _____ as an Customer Care Representative I did not understand the system for recording customer returns resulting in problems with stock reconciliations. The accountants discovered the error quickly and managed to fix the problem. For me though, it was a lesson that I never forgot and ever since I make sure I know company procedures in depth and follow them to the letter.*

Losing Answer

> *"I never made a mistake" or "I never make mistakes"*

We just don't believe these answers and when we hear then we probe deeper as it sounds as though the candidate is hiding something.

9.6 Decision Making

Q34: What types of important decisions are you required to make on a daily basis?

Q35: Describe your decision making process.

Q36: Tell me about a decision you would make differently if you had the chance.

Q37: What decisions are most difficult for you to make?

Q34: What types of important decisions are you required to make on a daily basis?

How to Answer

Every job holder will have a set of decisions to make on a regular frequency irrespective of the level of type or role. A senior executive may have to decide on spending millions on a new IT system while a secretary may have to decide when to order new stationery or book meetings.

The interviewer will be looking to see what you regard as an important decision and whether it is commensurate with your position. For example you may make decisions slightly above your level and while this would be regarded favourably making decisions clearly below your level would not.

Winning Answer

For me as a Customer Services Advisor the most important decisions revolve around how to provide fulfilment to customers who call to complain. I will work with the customer to understand their needs best and the options I have are to replace the product, issue a credit note for the same value or escalate the call to my supervisor. This would happen if the customer became abusive personally or if I had exhausted all options. I'm happy to say that very rarely do I have to refer a customer to my supervisor and I find that usually the customer is very happy with the decisions I make.

Losing Answer

I like to be involved with the day to day workings of the company and I will frequently make decisions about improvements to some of my managers' ways of working if I see that they are not successful.

This answer was given by the Head of Operations for a small bank and we concluded that this individual was afraid to delegate and trust their managers to do a good job.

Q35: Describe your decision making process.

How to Answer

Decisions are made at all levels and relate to all aspects of our daily and working lives and can include what to say, do, buy, etc. When dealing with the working environment there are a number of models available and the common elements of most are:

- Trigger – situation or problem requiring the decision
- Information - sufficient detail to be available
- Options - what are the choices
- Evaluate - check quality, assess the potential outcomes, including risks
- Implement - make the decision and put it into practice
- Review - How successful was it, is there a need to change

The interviewer is looking for you to demonstrate a clear decision making process, you should describe the steps you take and finish by describing a situation where you used your methodology successfully. If company policy or procedures dictate the process make sure that your answer shows you adhere fully to them.

Winning Answer

I represented the Head of Customer Care team on a project to deliver a new telephony system and I was responsible ultimately for the choice of solution. I started with a position statement on the current systems, assessment of the business plan and how telephony linked to this along with the related business drivers. I spent time researching the options taking professional advice on the most technical areas. I produced two estimates one of which I recommended and was accepted by the group.

Good detailed answer showing a competent decision making process which worked well in the given situation.

Losing Answer

When presented with a problem to sort out, I first ask other colleagues what they think the best solution is. I then see if this would work with my own ideas and come to a compromise solution that ensures the majority of people involved are happy.

Failed to show that a proper decision making process was followed.

Q36: Tell me about a decision you would make differently if you had the chance.

How to Answer

The interviewer is really asking 'Tell me about a mistake you made'. You are being invited to confess to a weakness and the options you when answering are:

- Say you don't recall any
- Mention something innocuous from an early part in your career and emphasise what you learned from the experience
- Choose a decision someone else made which did not work out and describe what you would have done, being careful not to criticise the individual involved

Winning Answer

In my first month with _____ I had some free time and decided to make some improvements to the monthly sales reports. They were very detailed and I had some great ideas which would make them much clearer to read and understand. I spent about two days and when done presented them to the Head of Sales for review. He was not pleased as he had designed the original report himself but after some time he did agree to incorporate some of my suggestions. In hindsight I would have approached him first for his go ahead before starting the task.

Losing Answer

Don't feel tempted to confess a decision which cost your company to lose significant amounts of money or other disastrous result.

Q37: What decisions are most difficult for you to make?

How to Answer

You can answer this question in a variety of ways depending on the level you are being recruited for. For supervisor or management levels the interviewer will be looking for evidence that you can make tough and possibly unpopular decisions and stand by them. Choose a situation where you had to dismiss a member of your staff for example or make a choice between two equally excellent job interview candidates. Provided you can articulate the process you followed and the rationale behind the decision your answer will be valid.

For entry level positions difficult decisions can be those which are one-offs and which you have not encountered before. Be very clear to show that you can think independently and refer to company policy and procedures and if in doubt escalate to a supervisor or manager.

Winning Answer

I recently had to make a decision to dismiss an employee I had recruited. I knew this person had great potential however their personal behaviour and actions were very clearly against company policy. It was a difficult decision on one level but I am very happy with the result as the morale in the team improved greatly once this person had left.

Losing Answer

It is important that you choose decisions which are not seen as part of your normal day to day activity, ones which are unexpected or unforeseen.

9.7   Persuading and Influencing

Q38: How do you go about persuading others?

Q39: Tell me about a time you had to negotiate with a supplier

Q40: Describe a time when you had to convince your colleagues that your views were right

Q41: Tell me about a time you were able to change someone's view completely.

Q38: How do you go about persuading others?

How to Answer

There are many techniques which can be employed to persuade and influence others. Key skills are, effective listening, communication, managing personal interactions, reducing resistance and conflict, building rapport and giving and receiving feedback. The interviewer will be looking for you to demonstrate your understanding of what's involved and examples of where you employed these skills successfully.

Example answers could include an activity or task you championed where initial support was not forthcoming from your colleagues but where over time you used your skills to get them on your side.

Winning Answer

I'm very aware of the importance of understanding others needs first and getting a clear idea of where they are coming from and what motivates them. As part of the process I try to build a relationship and create an atmosphere of trust and credibility and I work at getting them to buy into my views rather than forcing them.

This candidate then gave an example of where they used these skills successfully.

Losing Answer

I'm very busy in my role as Telesales Team Leader so I try to use my time as efficiently as possible. If I am persuading someone of my ideas I start off gently and become more forceful as I go along and by the end I generally have them agreeing with me.

Our conclusion was that while this candidate succeeds in persuading others it is only because they become over bearing and potentially aggressive and we did not feel that their core persuading skills were strong enough.

Q39: Tell me about a time you had to negotiate with a supplier.

How to Answer

Negotiation requires keen persuading and influencing skills irrespective of which parties are involved be they customers, suppliers, colleagues or managers. When answering, demonstrate that you used skills such as listening and understanding the suppliers' situation, communicating your companies needs clearly, stating your case competently and effectively and ultimately negotiating a win-win situation for both parties without any conflicts.

Winning Answer

I recently re-negotiated our telecoms contract with _____ and saved my company _____ per annum in the process. I prepared extensively prior to the meeting and knew exactly what we needed, I was confident they could deliver and my discussions were targeted at making sure that I achieved the best quality service at the best price possible. The sales manager was pleased also with the deal as they keep us a valued customer for another year.

Losing Answer

We negotiated a new contract with our stationery supplier this year and I'm happy to say we really screwed them on the cost. I think we got a great deal.

Firstly this candidate used 'we' suggesting they may not have had overall responsibility. Secondly, while they got a good price they did not demonstrate a positive relationship with their supplier which is essential in maintaining ongoing quality of service.

Q40: Describe a time when you had to convince your colleagues that your views were right.

How to Answer

Once again the interviewer is looking for clear evidence of your ability to persuade others.

Identify a situation that led to a positive outcome and talk about the particular skills you used to achieve the successful result.

Winning Answer

In my current job I redesigned internal processes for monthly agent performance reporting after agreement that the original system did not work very well. I set up a small group representing the major stakeholders and devised new procedures. Several internal departments did not agree with my proposals and it was my role to meet with them and persuade them of the advantages via a series of 1 to 1 and group discussions. I helped draw out the problems they were having and demonstrated how the new process would resolve them and in the end each internal department voted in favour of implementation of my ideas. I was very pleased with the result.

Losing Answer

If someone doesn't agree with my point of view I'll persuade them by meeting with them and talking about it. Generally where I have been leading a team my authority has allowed me to push through new practices however I'd like to think the staff all agreed with me.

This candidate did not seem skilled in persuasion and we got the impression that they relied on their position to force decisions through.

Q41: Tell me about a time you were able to change someone's view completely.

How to Answer

The interviewer is looking for evidence that you have the capacity and confidence to challenge pre-set ideas and using your imagination and initiative to effect a change in those views. You must show that you are willing and able to speak up for your own views and contribute when you know someone else is wrong.

We suggest it is better to choose a non-work related example if you have not experienced this type of scenario in your job. By saying you never had to persuade someone to change their mind may indicate that you are not very experienced or skilled in your interactions with others.

Winning Answer

I always express my point of view and if I know that someone else is wrong I will do my best to show them that it is so. This happened recently where I successfully convinced a colleague to divert resources to a project I was managing. I listened intently to understand their motivation and intentions and I asked them questions designed to get them thinking about different views. Questions such as 'What is the most important aspect for you?', 'What is your major concern relating to project B?' It took a number of meetings and phone calls but I was successful in the end.

Losing Answer

I find that people generally don't argue with me very often.

This answer was given by someone we felt was authoritative and aggressive and decided not to offer them the job as they would not have fitted with the team they would be part of.

Chapter 10

Role Specific Questions

This chapter looks at role specific questions. The first part answers questions for entry level applicants for jobs such as Customer Service Advisors, Call Centre Agents, Contact Centre Advisor, Customer Service Administrators, Customer Service Representatives, Customer Care Consultants, Customer Co-ordinators and Receptionists and Switchboard Agents.

The second section contains answers to questions for Team Leaders, Supervisors and Junior Managers and the final part of this chapter includes questions for Senior Manager jobs such as Head of Customer Services and Call Centre Managers. In addition candidates for these roles should expect to be asked any of the questions from the first part.

You will see that some of the questions are competency based and behavioural in style while others are designed to find out how committed you are to the interview process and how interested you really are in the position and the company. As over 80% of recruitment decisions are based on personality and fit we have included some questions which try to find out more about you as a person.

We would expect candidates to be asked a combination of questions from all the chapters in this book. Prepare and practice as many answers as the time frame will allow and use the interview scripts in Appendix I as a guide.

Customer Service Advisor and Other Entry Level Jobs

Q42: Why do you think you are suitable for a job in Customer Services?

Q43: What can you bring to the role of Customer Services Advisor that the other candidates cannot?

Q44: Tell me about a time you experienced stress in a Customer Care work environment.

Q45: How would you describe your personality?

Q46: How does your current Team Leader rate your Customer Service skills?

Q47: Describe a time in your last job when your handling of a customer was criticised.

Q48: Tell me about a time you disagreed with your manager.

Q49 Why did you choose to apply to our company, what was it that attracted you?

Q50: What do you know about our culture?

Q51: What would you say is a reasonable time to spend in this type of Call Centre job before moving on?

Q52: How ambitious are you and would you like to be a Team Leader or Supervisor?

Q53: How do you see your long term career plans in Customer Services?

Q42: Why do you think you are suitable for a job in Customer Services?

How to Answer

The interviewer wants to be convinced that you are capable of doing the job.

Refer to the job description and in your answer align 2 or 3 of the key competencies of the job to your own experience and past achievements.

In addition bring something extra that is inherent but not explicit in the job description, such as good communication skills, enthusiasm, systems skills etc

Winning Answer

I have always been interested in a career in Customer Care and really enjoy working in this type of role. I understand the job calls for someone with previous experience with strong communication and interpersonal skills. I am a Customer Care Advisor with four years experience with _____ in their call centre and one of my key strengths is my ability to deal effectively with all aspects of customer queries. I am dynamic, intelligent and have excellent keyboard skills and believe I can make a real contribution to this role.

Losing Answer

Well I'm very interested in people and I am proficient with many different software packages. I know most of these are not required in this job but I'm hoping to be able to integrate some of these into the role somewhere.

If the extra software packages are not key requirements of the job then it is not useful mentioning them. The interviewer may feel that the candidate has got their own agenda.

Q43: What can you bring to the role of Customer Services Advisor that the other candidates cannot?

How to Answer

Don't try to answer this question by comparing yourself to the other candidates as you have no idea what they are offering. However you do know the skill requirements from the job description, you know the desired characteristics from the person specification, you know from your research of the company what types of competencies they need and you know which of your skills and achievements are relevant.

Talk in terms of what you can bring to the role referring to relevant achievements.

Winning Answer

Its difficult to answer that question from outside your company, but I know that I can contribute _____ and based on my recent achievements at _____ where I managed a team of 15 Telesales Agents to deliver in excess of _____ of sales last year I know I can make a real contribution to this Performance Manager position

Losing Answer

I think I would be better than the other candidates because I'm sure I'm better qualified. I graduated from _____ University and I know that not very many people can say that.

This candidate came across as arrogant. Unless the interviewer is also a graduate from the same university this answer will do very little to help the candidates chances of success.

Q44: Tell me about a time you experienced stress in a Customer Care environment.

How to Answer

The interviewer is trying to see how you cope under pressure. The key here is to talk about an unusually stressful situation and show that you were able to solve the problem and thrive in a stressful environment.

Once again choose an example from a previous role which was a challenge. Briefly talk about the problem or situation and then in sufficient detail describe the steps you took to resolve it and finally finish off with a description of the successful outcome and its positive impact. Remember this is about what YOU did to resolve the situation, what steps YOU took.

Winning Answer

Dealing with customers is something I enjoy immensely and while I don't find it stressful as such I do enjoy the challenges it presents. A recent example was dealing with customers while we had a system outage which prevented us from accessing customer or product details on the computer. I used a manual system to record customer's orders and was able to give them the information they needed from product brochures and my own knowledge. When the system came back up I worked late to input all the orders so that the customers would receive their goods the next day. I regarded this as part of the job and was not bothered by it in any way.

Losing Answer

We had a power failure at work recently and I found it difficult to cope. We had a queue of customers but found that we could not deal with them properly and had to call them back later to finish the transaction.

While both candidates got the job done this one showed less initiative and seemed to lack the same quick thinking ability.

Q45: How would you describe your personality?

_____

How to Answer

This is not an invitation to ramble on about how bubbly and chatty you are and what a great sense of humour you possess. Rather, this provides you with a great opportunity to sell yourself and convince the interviewer you are the right person for the job.

Review your analysis of the job description, what are the key characteristics that are required? For example, common qualities include; Confident, Reliable, Dynamic, Focussed, Empathetic, Self motivated, Enthusiastic, Loyal, Determined, Results Oriented, a Team Player, Flexible, Customer Focused, Disciplined, Uses Initiative, a Problem Solver and a host of other 'positive' traits. Align those required in the job with ones you possess and you have your answer to this question.

Winning Answer

You can tailor your answer depending on the organisation and the culture but a balanced reply might be:

I have been described by my previous manager as reliable, determined and willing to work hard to ensure the job gets done. I thrive under pressure and am very keen to try new challenges. My friends would probably say that I am sociable, easy going, always ready to listen to others and willing to help out. I enjoy my work very much but also value my weekends and like to get into the country when I can.

Losing Answer

I'm a really jolly person, get on with everyone and always ready to share a joke. I like being sociable and am always the lively person in the morning.

This candidate sounded like someone with whom it would be fun to socialise with on a Friday evening but not necessarily a very balanced person for the office.

Q46: How does your current Team Leader rate your Customer Service skills?

How to Answer

This question asks about your skills while simultaneously exploring your relationship with your previous manager. Refer to a recent performance appraisal or some form of feedback you have had which will back up your own assessment of your skills.

While it is possible that your previous supervisor/manager may not have rated your skills very highly and you may have had disagreements about it, we would suggest that you do not expand on this in the interview. In answering, find some aspects which your manager complimented you on and talk about those instead. Relate them to a particular achievement as in the example below.

Winning Answer

Well in my last appraisal I had some very positive feedback from my supervisor who was particularly pleased with the way I efficiently dealt with customer complaint calls.

This is a nice hook and be prepared to expand further as you will more than likely be asked to give more detail about this achievement.

Losing Answer

Well towards the end I was always arguing with my boss. She wasn't very good at her job and frankly I knew I could have done it better. That's why I'm here really, to get away from her.

Never criticise your previous boss or colleagues as this will only reflect negatively on you.

Q47: Describe a time in your last job when your handling of a customer was criticised.

How to Answer

This is a good question as it addresses a number of key areas all at once. It considers the possibility that your work was poor enough to be criticised, it looks at your tolerance and ability to take criticism and the interviewer will be looking for clues to see whether you still carry any emotional baggage from the experience.

As with previous negatively phrased questions, you have the freedom to just say 'I don't recall any incidents when that happened" and stop. This is fine however you could be dealing with an inexperienced interviewer and if you repeatedly give this answer you may come across as un-cooperative.

Winning Answer

I'm pleased to say that I never gave my previous boss cause to criticise me and in fact they only had good words to say about me and my performance.

Or

I don't recall a time when I was criticised, I am completely focused on making sure that my work is top quality.

Losing Answer

My boss didn't like the way that I greeted visitors. He said I was a bit abrupt and cheeky but I don't agree with him. I was just being friendly.

This was recorded in an interview for a receptionist position. Don't be tempted to turn the interview into a confessional; this will certainly lose you the job.

Q48: Tell me about a time you disagreed with your manager.

How to Answer

This question explores the candidates' relationship with a current or previous manager, their attitude to authority in general and their willingness to challenge and stand up for their own opinion.

On one level their answer could reveal ongoing issues and weaknesses which are yet to be resolved while on the other could show the candidate to be confident, articulate and able to persuade others of their point of view.

This is not an invitation to complain or criticise your supervisor. Rather we recommend choosing an example where both parties were left in a positive light but demonstrating that you were able to argue your case effectively.

Winning Answer

This happened very rarely because we had very similar thought processes. I do remember a situation which related to my decision to deal with a customer call in a particular way. I knew from the company's procedure manual that we were not allowed to give refunds over _____ however the customer insisted that I give more. My supervisor took the call and agreed to the customers request and while I respected their decision I did not agree with it as it was outside of agreed policy.

Losing Answer

My boss and I rarely disagreed because I learned early on which areas we did not see eye to eye on. Consequently I used to try to avoid disagreements by resolving them myself without resorting to my boss.

We felt that this candidate showed a well meaning but deceptive nature and a tendency to avoid rather than face up to difficult or uncomfortable situations.

Q49: Why did you choose to apply to our company, what was it that attracted you?

How to Answer

Make note that this question refers to the company rather than the role itself. There are some organisations which offer opportunities in terms of advancement which others cannot. Some of the larger firms are often seen as springboards for graduates especially, to get into Team Leader and other management positions. For other candidates the attraction may lie in the products, the location, the sector and the values of the organisation.

Overall, the interviewer will want to hear that you made a positive choice to target their company, that you believe you will fit in and that this is where your future career lies. You need to demonstrate that you've researched the market place and selected this company as the one where you can contribute.

Avoid mentioning the great salary package, fast car or long holiday arrangements that come with the role.

Winning Answer

Once I made the decision to move on from my current role, I researched the market place and the companies advertising at this level. Yours not only offers a position where my experience fits directly but also has a good reputation for career development and strong performance, both of which are important to me.

Losing Answer

Well, I've been looking for a new job for a while and haven't had any offers so I thought I'd try a different direction. I need a job near to where I work too and I've always thought I'd be good in this sort of role.

Not a very strong answer and did not show a positive choice to target this particular company. This type of candidate would be more likely to leave the position quicker.

Q50: What do you know about our culture?

How to Answer

This could be a difficult question to answer unless you have had first hand experience of the organisation. Refer to any research you have done and remember that generic characteristics of most companies include: strong work ethic, value customers and staff, deliver good results, preferred employer, etc.

Do try to indicate that even if you don't have all the detailed knowledge you believe that you will fit with the organisation. Use this as an opportunity to ask about the culture as this will help you decide whether in fact the company is right for you.

Winning Answer

Looking at your website, I can see that the culture is about customer service first with strong emphasis on back-end support for the staff to ensure they can deliver. You highlight career development in your job adverts which gives the impression of working with staff to maximise their potential and allowing them to do great jobs and this is important to me too. I'm looking for a company which really delivers on staff support and training and also spends time working to deliver what the customer wants and I think from what I've seen your company does this. Can you confirm my thoughts on this?

Losing Answer

I know you also have quite good benefits and that's appealing and I'd hope the culture was one where I could be myself and feel comfortable.

Reasonable answer but does not demonstrate any active research and showed the candidate to be more interested in what the company was going to do for them rather than the other way around.

Q51: What would you say is a reasonable time to spend in this type of Call Centre job before moving on?

How to Answer

This is a very direct question aimed at finding out what your view of a 'reasonable time' is. A generally held opinion is that a period of 2-5 years in one position is reasonable. Any shorter would suggest lack of commitment and any longer a lack of ambition.

If this is your first job, you are free to give a stock answer talking about long term career, personal development, continuing to contribute in a challenging role, considering promotions as and when they become available etc.

If however your CV or Resume shows that you have moved jobs frequently you will have to work harder to convince the interviewer that this position is different. Cite the reasons for leaving previous jobs as per questions 2, lack of advancement opportunity, need for challenge, stability and location. You must reassure the interviewer that you are worth spending their time on in terms of the interview process, appointment, subsequent training and career development.

Winning Answer

People often move jobs regularly and there is sometimes an impression that this is the thing to do however I'm looking for a position that I can develop into and a role that can grow with a company where I can make a meaningful contribution.

Losing Answer

I think that moving jobs about every 2-4 years is normal these days and I tend to get itchy feet if I don't stick to that. I'm looking for a job from which I can get about 2 years good experience and then see what happens.

While this is a reasonably good answer and is true, the interviewer would have preferred to hear that the candidate intended staying in the role for a longer time.

Q52: How ambitious are you and would you like to be a Team Leader or Supervisor?

How to Answer

This is a tricky question to answer. If you say 'no' you may be perceived as lacking in ambition and drive and if you say 'yes' the interviewer may feel there is a risk that you would look to move on from the job sooner than expected. Be diplomatic when answering and try to achieve a balance. On the one hand you need to show a desire to develop your career, while on the other you need to convince the interviewer that you want to stay in the job for a reasonable period of time.

The key with this type of question is first and foremost to show that you are keen do a good job in the role being recruited for. You would like to develop within the department and the organisation and should an opportunity come along to step into your bosses shoes and you had the required experience and skills then you would be delighted to do so.

Winning Answer

My ambitions are very much about being the best at my job and the best Customer Services Advisor in your company and should an opportunity for advancement come along then I would be happy to consider it.

Losing Answer

Yes I am very ambitious and I would like to see myself get to the top of a large department within the next couple of years. I'm a bit of a go getter and I don't really allow anyone to stand in my way once I have decided to do something.

A key mistake is trying to be over confident or aggressive when answering this question as it may be seen as arrogant.

Q53: How do you see your long term career plans in Customer Services?

How to Answer

Similar in many ways to the question, 'Where do you see yourself in 5/10 years time?' the interviewer is keen to see where your career aspirations lie and whether they will take you away from this company.

Reassure the interviewer that your long term career is with their company and that you want to grow and develop under its guidance and roof.

Talk in general terms about continuing to make a meaningful and significant contribution to the best of your abilities. Show that you have analysed and considered your future career carefully and that the recruiting company is one in which you believe you could spend many years.

Winning Answer

I'm looking now to settle into a long term career with a large organisation such as yours and in the long term I would like to see myself developing and learning and contributing to your organisation to the very best of my abilities. I would like to be well regarded and respected by my superiors and should any opportunities for advancement come along within the organisation then I would hope to be in a position to consider those.

Losing Answer

A candidate needs to reassure the interviewer that their longer term plans include their organisation and this type of answer did not do so.

I don't know how long I will be in this job really and long term can't really promise anything. I'm very intelligent and I find that I need to have a lot of change going on to feel motivated.

Team Leader/Supervisor/Manager Level

Q54: Describe your management/supervisory style.

Q55: How do you get the best performance from your Call Centre Agents?

Q56: How would your previous subordinates describe you, what would they say?

Q57: Have you ever failed to meet your monthly targets and if so what action did you take?

Q58: Tell me about your recruitment experience within a similar Customer Service environment.

Q59: Describe a difficult situation you had with an employee and how you dealt with it.

Q60: Describe a situation where you had to reprimand or dismiss someone.

Q61: What is the most difficult aspect of being a manager or supervisor?

Q62: What methodologies do you find effective when monitoring Telephone Agents performance?

Q63: Tell me how you have used data to improve your team's productivity?

Q54: Describe your management / supervisory style.

How to Answer

Traditionally, management involves a combination of planning and organising and leading and supervising. The first two relate to the tasks and the second to the relationship with the people working for you and this direct question could be referring to your skill level with either or both. Before answering you may want to clarify with the interviewer which they are referring to.

In addition to capability and competence, the interviewer is looking for clues as to how closely your style fits with that of the organisation and the staff you will have working for you.

Winning Answer

In terms of people management, I would describe myself very much as a hands–on manager. I like to work closely with my staff in order to deliver maximum results and generate the best response both in terms of efficiency and morale. I think it's important to get to know and understand each member of the team and find out what their strengths are and where they need to develop. In terms of monitoring performance I prefer to use a system of performance management that includes regular appraisals linked to training programmes. I believe this style works very well as staff turnover in my previous two teams was 50% below the average in the industry.

Losing Answer

Well I'm quite easy to work for. I generally try and get a good team atmosphere going, taking staff out for a drink after work or something like that. I've not really had any problems with staff and I'm quite happy managing people.

This was not a good answer because firstly, it indicated that the candidate was relying on other people's goodwill to create a positive team spirit during an out of work period. Secondly it failed to convince us that they had dealt with performance management issues leading us to believe that they lacked the skills to do so.

Q55: How do you get the best performance from your Call Centre Agents?

How to Answer

A Supervisor or Team Leader will have a number of Agents to manage and in a Call Centre environment this number can range from 10-15. There are a number of methodologies and techniques that can be used to optimise performance including:

- Setting and communicating achievable targets
- Ensuring all agents are aware and accept targets
- Measuring and monitoring actual performance
- Bonus and incentive schemes
- Use of continuous performance appraisals
- Training, development and mentoring
- Equitable terms and conditions

Your answer could refer to some or all of the above and if you have used some specific tool to drive performance then talk about those also.

Winning Answer

I currently manage a team of 12 telesales agents and am proud that I increased my teams' performance by over 20% during the past twelve months. This I believe is due to a combination of instilling a real sense of team work, involving each member of the team in setting targets and ensuring that they 'own' those targets both as individuals and as a group. We have a bonus scheme with incentives based on targets met and exceeded and I use regular agent reporting to make sure that every one knows how well they are doing against plan. Finally I value regular performance management and ongoing training and development and all of this combined has really been successful for me.

Losing Answer

We have a bonus scheme in operation in the company and this seems to work well. I also have regular meetings and social events and this helps to create a really good team atmosphere.

This candidate seems to rely heavily of financial incentives and social interaction and this is not a good long term strategy.

137

Q56: How would your previous subordinates describe you, what would they say?

How to Answer

There are a variety of positive words that can be used to describe good management and leadership styles such as: motivational, caring, fair, open, good at delegating, effective communicator, getting results from the team, shares success with the whole team, supportive etc.

Winning Answer

I currently manage a team of four staff and I regularly ask for feedback on my management skills. They have described me as fair, committed and results driven and I'm proud to say that in my three years in this role I reduced absenteeism from 8% with my predecessor to only 2% now.

Using figures in this way is always interesting to an interviewer and the next question probed deeper and asked for more detail as to the steps this candidate took to improve those figures.

Losing Answer

I'm sure they would say that I am a fair but strict manager. I like to get things done and I don't have any patience with staff who come in late or make excuses. They are being paid to do a job and that's what they should be doing.

Probably the views of many managers but they should not be expressed in this way in an interview situation.

Q57: Have you ever failed to meet your monthly targets and if so what action did you take?

How to Answer

Because of the nature of Customer Services and especially in selling there will always be fluctuations. This can be due to seasonal issues, changeover in product types or a host of other issues which the sales person is dealing with. The interviewer is aware of this and is interested in seeing firstly if there was an extended period of low activity and if this ever recovered and secondly how you acted to improve your performance.

This question is phrased so that a 'no' answer could be given, however this is not useful to either party. In the selling profession a period of low sales could be seen as a developmental and learning opportunity and this is how we suggest you deal with this question.

Winning Answer

When I started selling mobile phones 2 years ago I did not reach my targets for the first 3 months. I did not understand why this was happening so I asked my manager to send me on a training course. I learned some great techniques to help me deal with customers both face to face and over the phone and in the first three months after the course I actually exceeded my targets. I was delighted and since then I generally meet or go over my targets.

Losing Answer

I never fail to meet my targets.

Might be true but could also suggest an exaggeration or that the targets are too low.

Q58: Tell me about your recruitment experience within a similar Customer Service environment.

How to Answer

The Call Centre or Customer Services Agent is often the first point of contact a customer has with the organisation and the experience can leave a positive or negative impression. It goes without saying that key to a successful Customer Services function is the recruitment of good quality staff. As a Team Leader or Supervisor part of your job will be the recruitment and training of agents and when answering you need to show an understanding of whats involved in the process. You would be expected to recognise the skills and qualities a good agent would possess and demonstrate your experience of hiring in this environment.

Winning Answer

In my current role with _____ I am responsible for the recruitment of Customer Care Agents. I work closely with the HR department and ensure that any decisions I make are in line with company policy. I have a detailed job description and person specification and each applicants CV is scored against this. I look for a broad range of expertise such as good communication and interpersonal skills and the interview process involves tests both written and verbal. When interviewing, I use a competency based system as this is a fairer and more accurate way of recruiting. Overall I find that I have recruited some excellent candidates some of whom have been with me for the past five years.

Losing Answer

In am very experienced in recruitment. During my career I have devised my own system of choosing candidates and find that this works for me. I look for eager and enthusiastic younger people as I find that they are easier to train and of course they are cheaper.

Much of this answer would ring warning bells for an interviewer. A lack of adherence to company policy, the focus on younger candidates rather than quality of skills could potentially breach legal requirements and a reliance on training as opposed to inherent skills or previous experience could prove costly in the long run.

Q59: Describe a difficult situation you had with an employee and how you dealt with it.

How to Answer

This question aims to discover how skilled you are at managing your staff. If you had experience of a particular problem with an employee, talk about it in terms of the successful outcome, demonstrating clearly the skills you used. Briefly describe the problem, talk about the steps you took to resolve it and articulate the result. Did you improve the motivation of the member of staff, reduce their absenteeism, improve their output?

Winning Answer

I had experience of a very difficult situation where one of my direct employees repeatedly made official complaints against a colleague. Being fully aware of the legal issues involved I made sure HR and the unions were involved from the start. I investigated thoroughly, met with both parties and presented my decision to HR and the unions. Both employees agreed to communication skills training which proved successful and with further mediation and training they now work very productively together.

Losing Answer

I rarely have problems with my staff. We get on very well both inside and outside of work and if any problems arise we just talk through them and resolve them between ourselves.

This may be a valid way of managing people and may work however as interviewers we were concerned that there was no reference to company policy in dealing with employee problems.

Q60: Describe a situation where you had to reprimand or dismiss someone.

How to Answer

These are common scenarios and it is all too possible that you may have had experience of one or both of these situations. The interviewer is trying to find out how good you are at managing people and how you coped with potentially stressful situations. Talk through one example and be positive about the part you played, the steps you took to resolve the situation, adherence to HR policy and legal doctrine. Mention the positive outcome for the company but also show sensitivity towards the member of staff.

Winning Answer

I did unfortunately have to fire one disruptive employee. I was very careful to involve the HR team in every step of the process and I made sure I followed company policy to the letter. I'm pleased to say that once this employee had left the morale in the department increased noticeably.

Losing Answer

I generally don't get involved where problems with staff are concerned. I just leave all that to the HR department and they get on with it.

Even in large organisations the manager must be involved in any disputes with employees. This candidate is either an incompetent manager or has not managed this type of situation previously.

Q61: What is the most difficult aspect of being a Customer Services Team Leader?

How to Answer

The interviewer is hoping that you will reveal some shortcoming in managing people. We suggest you choose a situation that is commonly regarded as difficult for all managers such as having to dismiss an employee or giving bad news to a team or individual.

Winning Answer

In my last role I was responsible for the re-organisation of the credit control team and as a result ten employees were made redundant. I did find it difficult giving these people notice however I was well aware that it was necessary for the overall survival and competitiveness of the organisation. We saved a lot of money and in fact many of those let go were pleased to get their redundancy package.

Losing Answer

Dealing with high staff turnover is a constant challenge for me.

It could be seen that this is a normal part of any managers or supervisors job and this answer suggested an inability to retain staff.

Q62: What methodologies do you find effective when monitoring Telephone Agents performance?

How to Answer

One of the main responsibilities of the Team Leader or Supervisor is to drive the performance of their team and ensure that targets are met. Most Call Centre telephony systems will have a built in monitoring system such as a wall board showing the number of calls answered and the % answered within 20 seconds and this will be updated continuously. In addition, there are automated and bespoke reports which can be generated during or at the end of the day showing performance figures for the individual agent, the team and the Call Centre.

There will be a system for recording sales and orders processed and these can be automated or created using a query builder. It is important when answering not only to describe the methodologies but show how and why they are effective and what actions you take to deal with poor performance.

Winning Answer

I use a combination of automated and specifically created reports to monitor performance. Some of the data comes from the IVR telephony system and other comes from the sales systems. Together they give me clear view of how each agent is performing on a daily basis against target. I find these effective as they allow me to address any performance issues almost instantly.

Losing Answer

I usually take a more informal view of monitoring performance. I find from experience that daily monitoring can have a de-motivational effect on the agents and I prefer to wait until the month end to assess productivity.

The previous candidate certainly showed a more professional attitude and one which would give an interviewer comfort that issues would be dealt with as they arose.

Q63: Tell me how you have used data to improve your team's productivity?

How to Answer

This could follow on from the previous question and the interviewer is looking to see how effective the candidates analytical and data interpretation skills are. It is all about using reports effectively and making the right decisions based on the data.

When answering, talk about the reports you receive whether from the telephony or sales systems or from another departments such as finance or HR. Show that you are able to analyse and assess and can take the initiative in making and implementing decisions which result in improvements.

Winning Answer

In my current job I devised a report to monitor cross-selling opportunities. Agents are given prompts from the system which will allow them to sell additional items and the reports I designed tell me how each agent is performing with each product. I have used these very effectively to identify top performers and those requiring additional training and by implementing a mentoring system I improved the overall performance of the team by over 20%.

Losing Answer

The systems in my last job were very poor and the reports I got were inadequate.

While this may have been true a candidate at this level would have been expected to use their initiative and create or devise reports which could be used.

Call Centre Manager/Customer Services Manager/ Head of Customer Services

Q64: Tell me about a change management project you were involved with which delivered successfully.

Q65: Now tell me a about a project you managed which failed to deliver.

Q66: We are considering introducing a new telephony solution. As a Call Centre Manager how would you see your role within the project team?

Q67: What key milestones do you envisage leading up to its successful implementation?

Q68: What are the key features you would you look for in a new telephony system?

Q69: What policies have you put in place to minimise attrition in Call Centre environments?

Q70: Tell me about the challenges you have staying within your budget

Q71: What approach do you take when preparing your annual budget?

Q72: What do you think about our products and is there anything you would suggest to improve them?

Q73: What do you see as being the greatest challenges to the Customer Servicing Industry?

Q64: Tell me about a change management you were involved with which delivered successfully.

How to Answer

Even if the project or task was a team effort, talk in terms of 'I'. Talk about how you interacted with the project team, customers, suppliers and management as appropriate. Give details about the part you played in the success of the project and if available quote numbers which will help give some idea of scale.

Mention the key steps involved when planning and defining the project and agreeing the end result, communication, the building of the business case, the governance and sign-off procedures, managing risks and issues, reporting and the exiting of the project.

As a senior manager you will be expected to show competence at all of these stages and if as a team member you will be able to describe the challenges you faced, the activities you undertook and the part you played in the successful delivery.

Winning Answer

> *Well I am particularly proud to say that I managed a project which saved my previous company _____ during a one year period.*

This statement had great impact and was a great hook. We then asked for more information and the candidate talked in great detail showing their competence and ease in delivering large projects.

Losing Answer

> *I helped out a team which in the end saved the company quite a bit of money, I'm not sure how much in the end, I wasn't really that close to the detail.*

This answer suggested that the candidate was on the fringes of some project and may not have had any direct impact.

Q65: Now tell me a about a project you managed which failed to deliver.

_____

How to Answer

This question will usually come after you have finished giving a good answer to the previous one. You may be feeling confident and secure and the interviewer is hoping you will reveal an inadequacy.

You don't have to answer in the negative and it is acceptable to say "I'm pleased to say this has never happened to me" and then expand on some positive aspect of the situation.

Failure to deliver can relate to overspending, not completing on time or the end result not functioning as agreed upfront. As an alternative you could talk about a smaller project you managed in the early stages of your career which did not deliver on one of these fronts and from which you gathered life enhancing experiences and learning. Be aware that once you admit to a weakness the interviewee will probe deeper to see if you really have conquered it.

Winning Answer

I don't recall a time when a project I managed did not deliver. For me priority is all about getting the project done on time and to the agreed specifications and I am always very cautious about controlling spending. In this way I was able to deliver a major system upgrade at _____ last year within the time frames which saved over _____.

Losing Answer

Sometimes it just can't be helped if a project goes over budget. After all, that's what the contingency is there for.

This candidate may have been expressing the views of many project managers but this answer did not give us comfort that they were competent at managing spending.

Q66: We are considering introducing a new telephony solution. As Call Centre Manager how would you see your role within the project team?

How to Answer

Most project methodologies will have similar structures in terms of the people involved and the roles they play in delivering the end result. For example PRINCE 2 a UK Government sponsored system, states that every project should have a Project Board which will have a representative from the customer, the end user and possibly from the supplier. There will be a Project Manager and who reports to the Project Board and who manages the day to day running of the project.

As Call Centre Manager your role would be as customer or end user and your responsibilty will be for ensuring that the end result meets with your requirements. You will make decisions on spending and timing and will sign of progress at selected stages.

At this level it is important to recognise that you would not act as a Project Manager and will employ an expert who can do so.

Winning Answer

> *As Call Centre Manager I would be involved from the very start of the project and would be instrumental in choosing the most effective solution. I would take the role of both customer and end user and would be responsible for signing off the initial business case, for appointing the project manager, for agreeing the specification and for ensuring that the end user matches the agreed requirements. I am pleased to say I was involved with a similar project at _____. Would you like me to talk more about that?*

Losing Answer

Be wary of assuming too much of the day to day control of the project. This should be left to the Project Manager who will report regularly to the Project Board.

Q67: What key milestones do you envisage leading up to its successful implementation?

How to Answer

Following on from the previous question you would be expected to talk in detail highlighting the process you would follow in delivering the project and the key milestones you would put in place. Give a fully comprehensive answer and refer to previous projects you have worked on demonstrating your competence and capability.

Winning Answer

The trigger point for me and the first key milestone would be the completion of a current state assessment, an analysis of the current system, its features, its advantages, its shortfalls and a full specification of what we are looking for in a new system. Second milestone would be to conduct a review of available systems in the market place, assess their suitability and benchmark against our competitors. Once a decision is made additional milestones would include the appointment of a project manager and project board, creation and sign off of a business case, time tables and implementation plans, training of users and ensuring that a disaster recovery plan is in place.

You can then relate this to a particular project you delivered in a previous role as this will bring the subject to life and make it easier for the interviewer to see that you are capable.

Losing Answer

You will really only be able to speak from experience with this type of detailed question. It is best not to try and bluff.

Q68: What are the key features you would you look for in a new telephony system?

How to Answer

This is a highly spoecialised question but one that a candidate for a Call Centre Manager position should be able to answer. An effective telephony system is at the heart of most Customer Services operations and key features of a top class solution will include:

- IVR – Interactive Voice Response, automatic channeling of calls
- ACD- Automatic Call Distributors, manages inbound call volumes
- CTI – Computer Telephony Integration, linking into systems such as the internet
- CRM- Customer Relationship Management, ability to update customer databases in a live environment
- Call Recording
- Scaleable and upgradeable
- Solid maintenance contracts
- Suppliers research and development programmes
- Cost effectiveness

Winning Answer

Talk fluently and confidently using some or all of the features above and if you have particular experience then refer to this also.

Losing Answer

As with the previous question, you will have knowledge of this or not and it is best not to try and bluff as you may be asked detailed technical questions relating to any aspect of your answer.

Q69: What policies have you put in place to minimise attrition in Call Centre environments?

How to Answer

Staff turnover is an ongoing problem in Customer Services and especially in Call Centre environments. This runs at anywhere between 20%-30% and is a constant challenge for managers.

Efforts to reduce this starts with the recruitment policy and with our 3Cs of capability, commitment and cultural fit. Firstly, there is a need to filter out those candidates who do not have the necessary knowledge, skills or abilities to perform to a satisfactory level. Secondly, it is key to identify candidates who do not have the intention of staying with the job for a foreseeable period and finally, the process should identify those candidates whose natural behaviours or work styles conflict with the nature of the company.

Once recruited, it is important to give sufficient training, monitor productivity, involve staff in setting targets, conduct regular appraisals, encourage a sense of teamwork and achievement. It may be that a flexible work life policy, setting rotas that suit staff and providing a decent working environment can help.

Winning Answer

Use any of all of the above in your answer and refer to previous experience where appropriate.

Q70: Tell me about the challenges you have staying within your budget

---

How to Answer

Cost pressures are a constant factor in business today where there is an ongoing need to maximise efficiency and reduce costs to stay competitive.

Any budget holder will be familiar with this and cost reduction challenges can be internally generated or come from higher up the organisation. In your answer demonstrate your understanding of this and importantly show that you can work to meet these challenges.

In addition there will be unexpected events that occur whereby a decision has to be made to spend more money or risk non-delivery and the interviewer is looking to see how well you rise to these challenges and what steps you take.

Winning Answer

I am well aware of the importance of staying within my budget and reducing costs where possible. I make sure that every member of my team is aware of the budget limitations and that any unnecessary spending is eliminated. I have an ongoing programme of cost reduction whereby each member of the team can make suggestions to improve productivity and reduce costs. These are reviewed and if appropriate implemented with the team member getting credit for the savings made. This helps to improve morale also.

Losing Answer

We do find it difficult to stay within budget, especially if some unplanned for event occurs. We would take funds from one area of the budget to cover this and then look at ways that we can save afterwards.

While this happens very often, it might have been better to say that when the unplanned for event occurred, the whole of the budget was revised and cost savings identified in advance rather than doing so retrospectively.

Q71: What approach do you take when preparing your annual budget?

How to Answer

Typical steps when creating a budget include:

- Review of current year and last year spend
- Gathering information relating to future projects, events, product launches, increase or decrease in staff levels and any other changes to operations
- Analysing and assessing the chance of implementation or occurrence
- Preparing a detailed schedule of costs with clearly stated assumptions and calculations
- Review and compare to current
- Revise as necessary
- Submit for approval and sign off

If you have experience, give a straightforward answer detailing the steps you take. Show that you are aware of the importance of involving the finance team, your managers and other relevant technical experts. Make sure you meet your submission deadlines and that your budget is in the format required.

Winning Answer

Our finance department will issue instructions in October and I have 3 weeks to complete and submit my first draft. In reality I have been planning well in advance so completion take a lot less time. My three managers will have completed their own team budgets and my task is to consolidate and review. If I see an area of unusual expenditure or greatly increased cost I will query this and may reduce it. Once submitted I am then closely involved with all reviews and changes.

Losing Answer

In your answer, show due regard for the review process and the need to adhere to overall company policy on spending.

Q72: What do you think about our products and is there anything you would suggest to improve them?

How to Answer

This is a threefold question:

1. If you are really keen and genuinely interested in winning the job you will have researched the company and its products in detail. This is what the interviewer is trying to discover as it will indicate if you are likely to respond with a yes should they make an offer.
2. Your answer could give clues as to the strength of your analytical skills and you may be in a position to offer some valuable advice, however it is best not to criticise the products in any way.
3. This could also be used as a test of your ability to think on your feet and see how creative you are. The interviewer might add that there are problems with one product and could ask your advice as to how to solve them.

Winning Answer

Before I made my application I had a look at your website and I think your products are very well matched to customer demand but I don't have enough detail to make any suggestions. Your accounts also show a very positive picture and give confidence of a secure company to work for which is exactly what I am looking for.

Losing Answer

From what I have heard, you sound like a good company to work for and I think you've been around for a few years so your products must be meeting customer demand. I've not worked in this industry before but I'm a quick learner and I'm sure working here will not be a problem for me.

This answer did not demonstrate any active research on the candidate's part and they appeared to be relying on hearsay for their information. We wondered how keen they really were on the position.

Q73: What do you see as being the greatest challenge to the Customer Servicing Industry?

How to Answer

At this level you would be expected to speak about the Customer Services Industry with some fluency. You will either have progressed through the ranks and are looking for a promotion or will be transferring from another sector. Either way we recommend that you carry out some research into the industry and are able to quote facts and figures. Chapter 1 contains some useful information including an analysis of the different issues facing the industry at the present time.

Winning Answer

I have worked most of my career in the Customer Services sector and am aware of the challenges such as high staff turnover, the lack of suitably qualified management, ongoing cost challenges. Of course more recently we have seen the increase in the trend towards outsourcing which in my opinion is both an opportunity and a threat and I would this see as the greatest challenge. I have been involved in migrating my past cost centre function to India and am happy to talk in more detail about that should you wish.

Losing Answer

Be specific when answering and show your personal experience of the issues. This will be more convincing than a discussion in general terms only.

Chapter 11

Tough Questions for All

The questions in this chapter can be difficult to answer, can put the candidate in an uncomfortable position and can even come as a total surprise. Some may be asked as standard towards the end of the interview while others would be asked if the candidate appeared to be cocky or over rehearsed.

They can come in any form, direct, open and closed and they will all be designed to see how you cope under pressure. They will be a test of your ability to think on your feet, to be spontaneous and targeted at encouraging you to open up more to the interviewer. Many of the questions we detail in the previous sections can also be regarded as pressure questions such as describing times when you had a problem or difficult scenarios you had to deal with.

Some of the questions in this section also deal with potentially uncomfortable period in your career especially if you moved jobs a lot, were made redundant or had gaps in your career. If this is the case for you, be prepared as the interviewer will feel duty bound to check the reasons behind these.

Other factors that may be deliberately manipulated to increase the stress factor on the day include awkward positioning of furniture, not allowing space for a coat or bag, either offering or nor offering a drink and using long silences in the hope that the candidate will ramble on and reveal some weakness. Our advice is to expect the unexpected and work with it. It is all part of the normal interview process and the key is to remain calm, composed and subjective without becoming defensive.

Q74: Talk me through your career progress to date.

Q75: Given the chance what would you do differently in your career?

Q76: I see you have been with _____ for 12 years. Do you think it will be difficult to adapt to a new environment?

Q77: Why were you made redundant?

Q78: Tell me about these gaps in your career.

Q79: How did your last performance appraisal go? In which areas could you have done better?

Q80: What areas of skills do you hope to improve upon over the next 12 months?

Q81: Tell me about an achievement you are particularly proud of.

Q82: Tell me about your education.

Q83: Why did you choose this university or college?

Q84: Why did you choose to study these particular subjects in school / university?

Q85: Your degree/qualifications are not relevant for this role. Do you see that being a problem?

Q86: What other roles have you considered and why?

Q87: How did you prepare for this interview?

Q88: If you don't get this job what will you do?

Q89: What do you like to do outside of work?

Q90: What else should we know about you?

Q91: What is your view of flexible working and work life balance?

Q92: Can we check references?

Q93: Do you have any holidays booked? / What is your notice period?/ When can you start?

Q94: Do you plan on having children?

Q95: Are you willing to travel? / Are you willing to relocate?

Q96: Based on what you have heard so far, how do you feel about the job?

Q74: Talk me through your career progress to date

How to Answer

This is a great question from the interviewees' point of view. It is an open question which allows you to provide a historical perspective of your career to date and at the same time gives you an opportunity to talk about your current or latest role in more detail.

The interviewer will be looking for evidence of;

- Well thought out and deliberate planning
- Progressive and well measured promotions
- The taking on of increased responsibilities
- Recognition and reward by previous employers
- Well conceived moves to new organisations either upwards or sideways
- Learning and development at every stage
- Consistency in terms of subject
- Some connection between job moves

Winning Answer

The interviewer will also want to see the logic behind your move to their company and if it is part of a seamless path you will be more likely to receive an offer than if it is a jump into the unknown.

Losing Answer

Even if you have stayed in the same position for many years you will be able to talk through the variety of tasks you performed during that time, the increased level of expertise you acquired and the learning and development you undertook.

Similarly, moving from job to job in the same company is highly valuable provided you can show progress from one to the other.

Q75: Given the chance what would you do differently in your career?

_____

How to Answer

Imagine the scene, you have given a great answer to the previous question, talked through your career to date with confidence and assurance and then the interviewer asks this question immediately afterwards.

You might be tempted to admit that maybe your decision to move to XY Company was not the best thought out or did not end up as rewarding as you expected. Resist the temptation however; the interview room is not the place to admit to mistakes or inadequacies of any kind.

Feel free to answer with a simple, 'Nothing'.

Winning Answer

Nothing. I am very pleased with my career to date, I have enjoyed it immensely and I am hoping to carry on making a meaningful contribution in my next position.

Losing Answer

I would have left _____ Bank sooner. I learned very little during my last 2 years there.

This candidate did not do themselves any favours by admitting to this failing.

Q76: I see you have been with _____ for 12 years. Do you think it will be difficult to adapt to a new environment?

How to Answer

This is a potential question for those who may have been with the same company for a long period of time or who have only been with one organisation their entire career to date.

The key is to talk about transferable skills which are common to all industries and companies such as excellent interpersonal and communication skills, team work, decision making but of course relate them to the requirements of the role being recruited for.

Talk about the range of jobs you may have had in the same company and the variety of activities you had to carry out. Explain that your reason for staying was because there was always a new challenge and a new skill you were able to acquire.

Winning Answer

I don't believe it will be a difficult. I had a variety of different jobs with _____ and being such a large organisation each job felt as if I was moving to a new company. Each part had different ways of working and I acquired a great range of skills which I know I can use to contribute to this role.

Losing Answer

_____ gave me a secure and interesting job for the past 12 years and I'm sure that your organisation will do the same."

It's not about what the recruiting company can do for the candidate but the other way around and this candidate came across as being too needy.

Q77: Why were you made redundant?

How to Answer

In the current business environment of aggressive mergers and acquisitions and ongoing internal re-organisation there is NO stigma attached to being made redundant. In fact it is not uncommon to meet people who have been made or chosen redundancy more than once and found it a career enhancing move.

The key point to remember is that it is the job that is made redundant or has been displaced. You as an individual have not and all your skills and experience are highly valuable. When giving your answer turn this into a positive move, one where you made a choice.

Quite often however being made redundant is a traumatic event and many people react negatively. The interviewer will be trying to find out how you handled the situation and if you have recovered emotionally.

Winning Answer

I had a very successful time with the company and was promoted a number of times. I realised however that future opportunities were limited so when the chance for redundancy came about I decided it was time to leave and develop my career further elsewhere. I indicated to my manager that I was willing to accept and feel lucky to have been chosen.

Losing Answer

I worked for that company for 15 years and then completely out of the blue they got rid of me. They said they were having a restructure but I think they just wanted to replace us with cheaper younger managers. I don't think I will ever forgive them for what they did.

This answer clearly showed that the individual was still suffering emotionally from being made redundant. Few employers would be willing to take on someone with this frame of mind.

Q78: Tell me about these gaps in your career. (Why were you out of work or unemployed for so long?)

How to Answer

If you have taken time out of your career and the interviewer wants to know more about it, make sure your answer is positive and shows the learning and development that took place during the gap period. For example having and rearing children is a life enhancing experience and one which can be used in a work environment. Ask any parent who needs to get kids to school in the morning and they will tell you that you need top organisational, team working and negotiation skills!

A career break to travel, shows imagination, initiative and drive, all qualities which are highly regarded in any organisation. Similarly by studying or running a business even an unsuccessful one you will have gained additional skills which can be used to contribute to any role.

Winning Answer

A gap may also be due to difficulty in finding a new position and a suitable answer in this situation is:

I decided to take some time in finding my next job as I want to settle into a long term career where I can use all my skills to make a real contribution.

Losing Answer

I have been having problems getting a new job. It is just not easy to get motivated and I think part of the problem is I'm not sure what I really want to do.

This candidate will fail to convince the interviewer that they are serious about this position and intend staying in the role for a reasonable time.

Q79: How did your last performance appraisal go? In which areas could you have done better?

How to Answer

Many companies operate an employee appraisal system with some holding annual reviews and others having reviews every one to three months. These assess the staff members' performance against a range of pre-set targets and goals as well as addressing behavioural and learning and development issues. Some methodologies also give the employee an opportunity to comment on their own performance too.

When answering, focus on the positive. Be honest as your new employer will ask for references and these may refer to performance issues experienced. If this is the case treat them as development opportunities, areas that you know you need to improve on and show that you are taking a course of action to rectify.

When talking about areas in which you could have done better refer to them in terms of personal goals rather than those imposed by your boss. This will show you to be a self starter, keen to change and highly motivated.

Winning Answer

I had a very good appraisal and overall was very pleased with my progress over the course of the year. I am working to improve my computer skills and am taking evening classes to get me up to speed and do not intend for this to be an issue in the near future.

Losing Answer

My appraisal was rated as good but I believe it should have been scored at excellent. I raised the issue with my boss but did not have a satisfactory response.

It is common to have disputes over ratings as appraisals are based on the views of each individual. It is best not to mention these disputes in the interview as they will reflect negatively on you.

Q80: What area of skills do you hope to improve on over the next 12 months?

How to Answer

This is an interesting and complex question putting the candidate in a bit of a 'catch-22' situation. If they admit to the need to improve on some aspect of their skill base they could be eliminating themselves from the running, especially if that is a key requirement of the job. If they say there are no areas for improvement, they will come across as lacking in self–awareness, a desire to grow and possibly show conceitedness.

There is always room for improvement and the key is to choose an area that is not crucial to being able to do the job competently. Similarly, be careful not to take a problem with you to your new employer. Show that you have taken the initiative and are already working to make the necessary changes.

Winning Answer

I realise that my ability to make presentations is not as good as I would like so I am taking a 'Presentation Skills' course provided by my local adult education institute. This will finish in the next 6 weeks and I am confident I will be much improved by then.

Losing Answer

I am hoping to improve my presentation skills ability and hope you have some training I can take advantage of.

Not an encouraging response.

Q81: Tell me about an achievement you are particularly proud of.

How to Answer

Choose an achievement that is recent, that you do feel proud of and importantly that is relevant to the job being recruited for.

The interviewer will be looking for confirmation that achievements shown on your CV or Resume are true and they may ask you to talk in more detail about a number of these.

Prepare and practice an answer to all the major achievements on your CV/Resume, use 'I' rather than 'we' and follow the **iPAR** structure:

- Talk about the part you played in IDENTIFYING the problem
- Describe the PROBLEM, challenge or situation
- Describe what you did to resolve it, the ACTIONS you took
- Detail the successful RESULT and use figures to illustrate.

Winning Answer

> *A recent achievement I am particularly proud of is where I identified issues with our IVR system where the customers were being channelled to the wrong department. I had a number of comments from customers which I decided to investigate and after some analysis discovered the problem. I advised my Team Leader and together we approached the IT department who were able to fix the problem very quickly. I feel proud of myself and know that it has saved us getting lots of negative comments from customers.*

Losing Answer

Don't talk about an achievement that is not on your resume. This will make the interviewer question just how true it is and they may conclude it is fabricated.

Q82: Tell me about your education

How to Answer

Quite simply the interviewer is looking for evidence of a required standard of education. Depending on the role, you will have been educated to a certain level and this is what you need to demonstrate.

Limit your answer to relevant studies and to those which are specifically stated as required in the job description. The interviewer will also want you to elaborate on what's stated on your CV/ Resume and link it with the job.

Winning Answer

I have the minimum requirement of _____ as stated in the job description. In addition, I graduated with a degree from _____ which gave me strong written skills and also taught me how to carry out detailed research. As these are key competencies of the role I'm sure my education will be of great benefit.

This is a good answer and one which shows that your education is relevant and of value to the role.

Losing Answer

"I went to _____ school for 8 years, then to _____ school followed by _____ University."

This repeats information which is clearly available on the Resume but does not give any additional detail as to why it is relevant to the job.

Q83: Why did you choose this university or college?

How to Answer

If this is your first job after leaving school or university the interviewer will use this type of question to get you talking about something you are familiar with.

At the same time the interviewer knows that the answer will reveal a lot about your mental processes in making a decision. They will be looking to see how much planning was involved and if this college was your first choice or not.

When answering, show that you had a clearly defined plan from early on, that you made a positive choice and you attained your goal. The interviewer will think that if you can apply these same characteristics in a work environment you are more likely to be a long term, productive and effective employee.

Winning Answer

I knew from an early stage in school that I wanted to go to _____ University. It has one of the best academic programs in electrical engineering and I worked very hard in my final year to make sure I had the grades to get in.

Losing Answer

I didn't have a particular choice in terms of the university I went to. I applied to several and got quite a few acceptances. I chose the one I though would give me the best degree.

Fine, but does not show the same level of determination and tenacity as the other answer would suggest.

Q84: Why did you choose to study these particular subjects in school / university?

How to Answer

The interviewer is looking for signs of a planned approach to your education and subsequent career and will be keen to see a relationship between your studies and the job being recruited for.

You need to show as far as you can that these have all been linked and form part of a structure rather than a haphazard approach.

The interviewer is also looking to see if you are genuinely interested in your field or just doing a job to get paid. Talk in some detail about why you like it and show that you are serious about your career.

Winning Answer

I chose to study business because it is a field I have always being interested in and know that my future career lies in this type of work. I enjoyed my studies and have an aptitude for sales management and it in this area I intend to specialise.

Losing Answer

I just followed my friends to university and did enjoy studying my subjects. Now I'm trying to find work using the qualifications I have although it's not easy sometimes.

This candidate did not seem to be able to make a connection between their studies and the job being applied for and were not specific about how the subjects, relevant or not could be used in the job.

Q85: Your degree/qualifications are not relevant for this role. Do you see that being a problem?

How to Answer

Colleges and Universities offer a whole range of degree courses few of which have much direct relevance to the work environment. Someone entering the legal profession with a degree in history and politics may never have encountered a law book during their studies and similarly many graduates with great degrees in art and design are happily working in banking, customer services and a host of non-related jobs.

The interviewer is well aware of this situation and asks this awkward question partly to see how you cope under pressure. The tone of the question could be taken as being critical or a negative reflection on your choice of subjects and subsequent career choice and it is important that you do not become defensive.

Talk about the 'transferable skills' you have acquired during your time at college or university which have set you up for a career in any field. Describe how key elements of your studies will help you contribute to the role and show your determination and enthusiasm towards this particular company and industry.

Winning Answer

An answer which overcomes the situation where a degree or other study may be perceived as irrelevant is.

> *I chose these topics because I felt that they would help me with my aim of working in a managerial capacity. Even though I did not study a business related subject I gained knowledge and experience of communicating, team working and making presentations which have so far all been very useful and I can see them being of real tangible benefit in this role.*

Losing Answer

> *My area of study is extremely beneficial and well regarded and I did get a first. I'm sure my skills will be useful.*

This candidate came across as a little defensive.

Q86: What other roles have you considered and why?

How to Answer

With this question the interviewer is probing to see if you are really interested in moving jobs, just looking around or trying to play one company off against the other.

Having made a decision to move it's quite likely you will have applied for several jobs and the interviewer will look for clues as to how high on the list their company and job is. They will want to see if the jobs you applied for are similar in nature, in the same sector or if you are just hoping to take the first that comes along.

They will not want to waste their time if your preferences clearly lie elsewhere so reassure them that they are your preferred employer and this type of job is what you are after. Mention that you would be delighted to receive an offer.

Winning Answer

I've spent time working out where I'd like to move to and have applied for a small number of specific roles. I am waiting to hear back from these interviews however am most interested in this role and would certainly accept if I received an offer.

Losing Answer

I've applied for quite a few as I really want to leave my current position. It's not satisfying me and there are issues at work.

This answer scared the interviewer into thinking the candidate did not fit in very well and were desperate to move to any job. There was real concern also about the 'issues' mentioned and they would have asked follow up questions to probe deeper.

Q87: How did you prepare for this interview?

_____

How to Answer

The interviewer will be keen to see how much work you did in advance as this will indicate your interest in the job.

Talk about the keys steps such as researching the company, analysing the job description and making sure your skills matched, conducting a mock interview, carrying out a trial journey, ensuring you had the right clothes etc. The more work you did the more comfortable the interviewer will feel that you are keen, it will show that you are self-motivated and determined and this will place you ahead of a candidate who did no little or no preparation at all.

You could extend your answer to include the application process and show that you have gone through a positive effort to get this particular role as opposed to just applying for any job.

Winning Answer

When I first made the decision to change jobs I spent time looking back on my Resume and thinking about the direction I wanted my career to go in. I've only applied for a few roles as I'm really keen to get the move right and chose a company and position where I knew I could make a meaningful contribution. I'm really keen to get the job offer and have researched your company and spoken to a contact I had who worked for you recently as well as looking at your web site and other online sources.

Losing Answer

When I first saw the job advertised I knew it was the one for me. It's exactly the sort of role I'm looking for and easy to get to work form where I live. I think I have the same sort of experience as you're looking for and the role will be easy for me to pick up.

There is a risk that this type of answer may come across as flippant and does not appear to have any real substance.

Q88: If you don't get this job what will you do?

___

How to Answer

The interviewer is looking for commitment and dedication to the role you are applying for and needs to be persuaded you are serious in your application. They want to see sufficient desire to win this job and work for this company without being overly desperate.

In addition this is a test of your ability to deal with rejection and overcome adversity so your answer should show a positive and upbeat attitude and a commitment to continue with your job search to get the one that is right for you.

Winning Answer

I would be very sorry not to get this role as I feel my skills are very well matched and this is the direction I want to take my career. If I don't get the job, I will think about why and I'd appreciate some feedback to help me with my next interview. I would certainly keep looking and re-apply should another suitable vacancy become available with your company.

Losing Answer

I'm applying for a few jobs at the moment so although I'd be sorry not to get this one I'm sure something else will come up.

This gives the impression of not being hungry enough for this particular role.

Q89: What do you like to do outside of work?

How to Answer

The interviewer is trying to find out more about you as a person. This will help them assess how well you will fit with the organisation. Our advice is to be honest and use this as a chance to demonstrate a rounded personality. Do not recite a long list of hobbies but try and show attention to and awareness of work-life balance.

Winning Answer

A thoughtful answer would be:

> *I enjoy my work thoroughly but I do make sure that I have sufficient free time to see family and friends. Generally I like being active and am quite sociable, meeting up with friends regularly at weekends. I am chairman of the local historical society and we meet weekly and plan activities and tours.*

This indicates an understanding that you need to have your own life but that it doesn't interfere with work i.e. going out at weekends, not weekdays. If you do work with any local groups, say so.

Losing Answer

> *I like swimming, jogging, reading, going to the theatre and eating out.*

Only mention genuine interests as the interviewer may share your views and could follow up with a detailed question about some aspect of that particular hobby.

Q90: What else should we know about you?

_____

How to Answer

This is an open question which is similar to 'Tell me about yourself'.

If it comes towards the end of the interview then it is an opportunity for you to talk a little more about your hobbies and interests outside of work. Be honest but restrained. Do mention any groups or societies you belong to and if you do any form of volunteer or community based work then talk about this also.

If there is an achievement you have not had a chance to talk about earlier then use this as an opportunity to sell yourself a little bit more.

Winning Answer

I haven't had a chance to mention it yet but I do volunteer work with the_____ Charity in my spare time. Every year I organise a fundraiser in my local area and last year I got over 16 firms involved and we contributed over _____.

This shows an ability to network, persuade others, organise teams as well as being interested in helping others.

Losing Answer

There's not a lot else to say really. I don't do very much outside of work bar watch football on TV and have a few beers with my friends.

Fine but you could sell yourself a lot more.

Q91: What is your view of flexible working and work life balance?

_____

How to Answer

Flexible working is very common in many firms and includes programmes like nine day fortnights, late in late out, career breaks and both maternity and paternity leave.

Be careful however with your answer. This could be a 'trap' as the interviewer may be keen to see whether you intend availing yourself of flexible working at some stage in the future.

If this is your intention do not mention it in the interview.

Winning Answer

> *I think it's a good idea and I can see how it would benefit certain employees and might help with morale and motivation. It's not something I feel I need to consider at this stage in my career.*

Losing Answer

> *I think work life balance is great and in my previous company I took a three month career break and travelled around the world. It's something I would like to do again. Does your company offer this?*

Not a good way to start a career with a new organisation even if they do have a work life policy.

Q92: Can we check references?

How to Answer

Although this seems a standard Human Resources question, the interviewer could be testing you to see if you left your last employer on good terms.

Winning Answer

A good answer would be:

> *My Resume shows referees from previous positions and also my current manager and personnel department. However, before you contact my current employer, please let me know in advance as its not common knowledge that I'm looking for work.*

Losing Answer

> *I haven't told my employer I'm looking for work so please don't ask for any references".*

Or

> *I can't give you any work referees but you can ask John Smith for a personal reference, he's someone I've known for a long time.*

Neither of these answers gives much confidence that the candidate has left on good terms from previous jobs or was highly regarded.

Q93: Do you have any holidays booked? / What is your notice period?/ When can you start?

How to Answer

Here the interviewer is hinting that your application may be taken further but bear in mind that these are also standard questions that are often asked of all candidates.

You should be honest at all times.

In terms of holidays don't make yourself appear inaccessible and equally don't give a detailed break down of your future travel plans, this is not what the interviewer wants to know.

Disclose your notice period and if it is greater than the standard one month you could look at options to reduce it through negotiation with your current employer or by taking holidays due.

Winning Answer

See above

Losing Answer

If you are out of work and asked about starting dates, don't at this stage say 'immediately' as this will give the impression that you are desperate and it may affect your ability to negotiate a stronger package. You can hint that you are waiting for answers from other interviews although you are very keen on this particular job.

Q94: Do you plan on having children?

___

How to Answer

In the UK, US and most countries a combination of the Race Relations Act, Sex Discrimination Act and other statutes forbid employers from discriminating against any person on the basis of sex, sexual orientation, disability, age, race, nationality, religion or disability.

You should not be asked questions such as:

Are you married?
How old are you?
Where were you born?
How many children do you have?
Do you plan on having children?
Etc

Despite these laws you may find that an inexperienced interviewer could innocently ask the above in some form or other. It is important that your do not get angry, upset or confrontational. Simply deal with the question honestly, naturally and move on.

Winning Answer

Should the interviewer persist you could always say "I'm not sure of the relevance of that question to the role" but best not to make an issue out of it.

Losing Answer

I have never been asked such a question before and I am very offended. I know it is illegal to ask this and I may consider taking legal action against you.

This will certainly not endear the candidate to the interviewer.

Q95: Are you willing to travel? / Are you willing to relocate?

How to Answer

You should know in advance if travel is involved in the role or if the company will be requiring you to relocate. Even if this question comes as a complete surprise keep cool and as with the previous question show enthusiasm and interest and reflect outside the interview room.

It maybe that the interviewer is testing to see how your commitment would hold up in the event that the company decided to move even though it is not planned.

Winning Answer

I am very keen on this job and willing to do whatever it takes to do the very best job possible.

Losing Answer

I did not realise that relocation was a requirement. I would have to think seriously about accepting the job if that was the case.

Once again this might suggest that the candidate is not interested.

Q96: Based on what you have heard so far, how do you feel about the job?

How to Answer

This is an interesting question and one which could very well be asked at the end of the interview. It is another 'green light' type question and while it may indicate that the interview has gone well it could be just a standard question asked of all candidates.

The interviewer is trying to see if your views about the job have changed, if it is less or more attractive than originally perceived. Ultimately the interviewer will not want to waste time making an offer to someone who is not going to accept and they would prefer to know earlier rather than later.

Our suggestion is to answer in a positive and enthusiastic manner. While you may have doubts, it is best to keep your options open and take some time to reflect outside of the interview room. If you are offered a position you can always say no.

Winning Answer

Thank you for seeing me today and I am even more convinced that I can bring something special to this role and to the organisation. I would be very pleased to receive an offer and am excited to get started as soon as possible.

Losing Answer

It all sounds good but I need to go away and think about a couple of issues that we discussed.

This answer may indicate that the candidate is not interested.

Chapter 12

Questions for BPO Candidates

Business Process Outsourcing or BPO as it is more commonly known is the activity of transferring some of an organisation's business processes to an external provider. The rationale behind this strategy is that the outsourcing partner can effectively carry out what is usually a repetitive non-core process such as Customer Servicing while leaving the head organisation to concentrate on what it does best, be it selling, manufacturing etc.

The most common business process that gets outsourced is call centers. Over the past five years a variety of top companeis have outsourced to low waged, English speaking countries in Asia and Latin America. A highly educated workforce and low wages have made India one of the most common destinations and banks, telecomes and retailers have all have moved call centre functions to cities such as Mumbai, Bangalore and Bombay. Modern tecnhological resources and state of the art facilities have also attracted US and UK IT companies to outsource their help desks and many software and hardware queries are now answered many thousand of miles away by highly competent graduates.

For many in these countries a career in BPO is a lucrative and secure one. It is highly competitve with many graduates chasing the same roles especially with the top organisations.

Key skills required by BPO job interview candidates include:

- Excellent command of the outsourcing componeis language usually English
- Excellent communication skills both written and verbal
- Interpersonal and people management skills
- Keyboard and computer skills

In addition some comaonies will insist on experience in a customer care or telephony environment and there will be a minimum educational standard required.

In addition to all of the previous questions mentioned in this guide we would expect specific questions to be asked as follows:

Where did you learn your English?
How would you rate your level of English?
Which is better, your written or spoken English?
What plans do you have to further improve your English?
What do you know about the culture of _____ (country)?
What is a popular television programme in _____?
What do you know about the polictical situation in _____?
Who is Prime Minister/President?
What newspapers and magazines do you read?
What is your understanding of the banking system in _____?
What is your experience of working in a voice-based BPO environment?
What would you do if you could not understand a customers accent?
What do you know about our company and what we do?
How long do you see your career in BPO?
Why did you choose to study those subjects in college/university?
How would you say your education will help in this role?

Many organisations do not publish the fact that their customer servicing is outsourced and the agent will need to have a convincing accent and knowledge of popular culture. Some companies include this as part of the initial training or induction however we recommend that you spend time researching the recruiting organisation, the sector and the country where its main customer base is located. Read newspapers, view web sites and generally get a feel for the culture. This will all go towards achieveing a succesful outcome to your interview.

Chapter

13

Closure: Including Questions to Ask

Ask Questions

As interviewers, we pay particular attention to the questions that the candidate asks us. Our experience shows that this says more about their interests and intentions than the answers they have given to our questions. For example if there are no questions being asked, we have to consider how interested this person is in the role. Are they here just for some interview practice or because an agency has encouraged them to come along. Either way we would probably not offer this candidate the role. An ideal candidate is one who asks intelligent, job related questions throughout the interview. They involve us in a discussion and come across as genuinely interested in the role and in the organisation. You can ask questions at any stage throughout the interview. This will not only demonstrate interest but will allow you to gather information vital to helping you decide if the job is right for you

The Company

These questions are designed to find out how strong and secure is the organisation, is it growing or not, are redundancies likely, is it your type of company.

- Can you tell me about the organisations plans to expand?
- What are your growth targets for next year?
- Do you have any new products you are expecting to launch next year?
- Do you have any plans to re-locate in the foreseeable future?
- Are you planning on increasing staff numbers in this particular department?
- Your accounts show a loss for the past year. How are you addressing this?
- What are your teams' goals and what can I do to contribute towards achieving those goals?
- What is your policy towards....?
- How would you describe the culture of the company?

The Role

- These questions are related to the job and can help clarify issues regarding the responsibilities and tasks involved.
- What are the key responsibilities of the job?
- What are the ongoing expectations of the job holder and how would you classify a great performer?
- What opportunities exist for growth and development in the role?
- How do you see me best contributing to the role with the experience and skills that I have got?
- Why is the position vacant?
- Why did the previous job holder leave?
- What are the immediate challenges in the role?
- What would you say is the one key think I could deliver which would benefit you and the company?
- What type of training do you provide?
- Can you describe the appraisal system?
- What would you say I could bring to role which would have the most immediate impact?
- Who does the job report to?
- Which of my achievements do you see being most relevant in the role?
- I thrive on managing large teams; do you see an opportunity for my team to grow in the future?
- What would it take for me to become a star employee?

The Interview Process

- These questions are related to the interview and recruitment process
- Would you like me to expand on any of my achievements?
- Can you tell me what happens next in the recruitment process?
- I'm very interested in the role, when do you expect to make a decision?
- Is there anything else you would like from me at this stage or prior to your decision?
- What else can I do to win the job?

Questions NOT to ask during an interview

We would recommend that you DO NOT ask the following in the interview. There will be plenty of time to discuss and consider these during the negotiation stage and after you have started working.

- How much will I get paid?
- How many days holidays do you give per year?
- Can I work flexi-time?
- Can I leave early on Fridays to take my children to sports practice?
- Do you give sick pay?
- Can I have travel expenses for this interview?

Or any form of the above. All of these may become relevant if you are offered the job and are not appropriate at this stage.

Follow Up

The last stage in the interview structure is **closure**. You will probably be about to breathe a sigh of relief that the interview is almost over however it is vital that you leave a strong lasting impression on the interviewers mind. Most candidates finish the interview by saying, "Thanks, bye". Sure this is polite but it does not make an impact.

As with your greeting, shake the interviewers hand, smile, make eye contact and say "I have enjoyed meeting you Mr Smith. I am very interested and excited about this role and I do hope to hear from you very soon"

On the way out use the small talk either with the interviewer or whoever escorts you from the building to communicate your interest. For example "It seems like a really nice office environment, I could certainly see myself fitting in here very nicely"

The interview may have ended but the interview process is not yet over. Very often it is the last candidate interviewed who actually gets the job offer and this is largely because the interviewer remembers more about them. If you are not at the forefront of the interviewers mind you will not be offered the job and this section is all about reminding the interviewer who you are.

Report

As soon as possible after the interview and possibly on the way home complete a report summarising the interview and include the following:

Names and titles of interviewer and anyone else you met
Your impressions of the job and the company
Where you think you performed well
Where you think you didn't perform well
What are the key competencies of the role?
What key strengths can you bring to the job?
What you would have liked to say but didn't

Letter

Within 24 hours of the interview close we recommend that you send a letter or email. Not only is this polite but it will also allow you to demonstrate that you are keen and to repeat why you think you are the right candidate for the job.

Keep the letter or email to no more than one page and use the following guidelines:
Mention how happy your were to meet
Reiterate why you think you are right for the job
Be enthusiastic and show that you are committed
Say that you are convinced that you will fit in with the company
Say how excited and happy you would be to receive the job offer

Phone Call

If you have not heard anything after a week we would suggest phoning the interviewer. They will have received your letter two to three days prior so your call may be timely. Be polite and do not appear to be pushing for a decision.

Say "I enjoyed meeting you and was hoping that you received my thank you letter. I just want to add that I am very interested in the role and believe I have the right skills and would very much enjoy being part of your team."

Making a decision may be difficult for the interviewer and your phone call may be enough to tip the balance in your favour, especially if the other candidates have not bothered making a call.

If nothing else the interviewer will remember you and should you miss out on this role you have an established rapport which may result in an offer for an alternative job at some later stage.

Respond

Despite all your efforts you may be turned down for the role. It may be that another candidate has some extra experience which was judged valuable and which you did not have.

The key here is to respond to the rejection letter. A short response thanking the interviewer and HR team for their time and re-iterating your interest and desire to work for that particular organisation.
Remind them of your skills and advise them that you would be delighted to be considered for any future position which becomes vacant.

It is possible that the winner of the job offer may turn it down and you might be next on the list. Alternatively in large organisations there is a continuous recruitment programme and you could find that you are offered a different role than that for which you interviewed.

You can at this stage ask for feedback on your interview performance and ask why you were not chosen for the role. Explain that you are keen to develop your skills and their comments will help with your future job search.

Review and Repeat

Now is also a good time to stop and review your performance so far. Use your post interview report and the feedback from the interviewer to assess how you are doing.

What went well?
Any negative points you need to consider
How did the interviewer perceive you?
Did you make a good first impression?
Do you need to practice your responses more?
Did you lose the job because of your experience as opposed to your interview performance?

There is a whole range of self analysis questions that you can ask and the key is to find and keep the good and change the not so good. If there are areas for improvement you need to develop a plan to change and use the techniques in the module as a guide.

If you have been rejected do not despair. It is very common for even the most qualified and best candidates to be rejected at some point in their careers. Many find on reflection that the job was not quite right for them and the rejection may have saved them years of stress trying to do a job for which they are not suited. Remember there is great job out there for you and it is simply a matter of time before you get that offer. Don't assume that because an interview went well that the job is yours. Continue with your job search even if you are waiting for a response from the interviewer and who knows you may have a selection of job offers to choose from very soon!

Index of Questions Answered

Common Interview Questions

Q1: Tell me about yourself
Q2: Why do you want to leave your current job?
Q3: What are your key strengths?
Q4: What are your weaknesses?
Q5: What do you like/dislike most about your current job?
Q6: Why should we select you for this job, what will you bring to the role?
Q7: Where do you see yourself in five/ten year's time?
Q8: What do you know about our company?
Q9: Why are you interested in this role and what is it that attracted you?
Q10: What is your Salary?

Competency and Behavioural Interview Questions

Customer Handling
Q11: Can you give an example of a time when you experienced good customer service and explain why it was good?
Q12: Tell me about a time when you gave effective customer service.
Q13: Describe the most difficult situation you encountered in customer services.
Q14: How would you respond if a customer called you to complain?
Q15: What characteristics are required in a good customer services advisor/call centre agent?

Communication
Q16: Tell me about a situation in your previous job where you used your communication skills effectively.
Q17: What experience do you have in making presentations and how do you rate your skills in this area?
Q18: In your current or a previous role what levels of management do/did you have to communicate with?
Q19: Do you prefer to communicate orally or by writing and explain why?
Q20: How would you rate your ability to communicate with senior management /colleagues/ customers/ subordinates?

Planning and Organising
Q21: How do you organise your time?
Q22: Imagine it is almost close of day and your boss gives you 5 urgent tasks to complete. What would you do?
Q23: Describe a time when you were unable to complete a task on time.
Q24: How do you plan and organise for long term tasks or projects?
Q25: Tell me about a situation where your planning skills let you down.

Team Working
Q26: Describe your team working skills and give an example of when these worked well.
Q27: Are you a team player and what role do you generally play in group situations?
Q28: What types of people do you get along with best and worse?
Q29: Tell me why you will fit with the team.
Q30: What experience have you had working on a team?

Problem Solving

Q31: Describe a difficult problem you had to deal with.

Q32: Working in Customer Services what types of problems do you resolve on a daily basis?

Q33: Tell me about a mistake or something you did wrong in your previous job.

Persuading and Influencing

Q38: How do you go about persuading others?

Q39: Tell me about a time you had to negotiate with a supplier

Q40: Describe a time when you had to convince your colleagues that your views were right

Q41: Tell me about a time you were able to change someone's view completely.

Role Specific Questions

Customer Service Advisor

Q42: Why do you think you are suitable for a job in Customer Services?

Q43: What can you bring to the role of Customer Services Advisor that the other candidates cannot?

Q44: Tell me about a time you experienced stress in a Customer Care work environment.

Q45: How would you describe your personality?

Q46: How does your current Team Leader rate your Customer Service skills?

Q47: Describe a time in your last job when your handling of a customer was criticised.

Q48: Tell me about a time you disagreed with your manager.

Q49 Why did you choose to apply to our company, what was it that attracted you?

Q50: What do you know about our culture?

Q51: What would you say is a reasonable time to spend in this type of Call Centre job before moving on?

Q52: How ambitious are you and would you like to be a Team Leader or Supervisor?

Q53: How do you see your long term career plans in Customer Services?

Team Leader/Supervisor

Q54: Describe your management/supervisory style.

Q55: How do you get the best performance from your Call Centre Agents?

Q56: How would your previous subordinates describe you, what would they say?

Q57: Have you ever failed to meet your monthly targets and if so what action did you take?

Q58: Tell me about your recruitment experience within a similar Customer Service environment.

Q59: Describe a difficult situation you had with an employee and how you dealt with it.

Q60: Describe a situation where you had to reprimand or dismiss someone.

Q61: What is the most difficult aspect of being a manager or supervisor?

Q62: What methodologies do you find effective when monitoring Telephone Agents performance?

Q63: Tell me how you have used data to improve your team's productivity?

Call Centre Manager/Customer Services Manager/ Head of Customer Services

Q64: Tell me about a change management project you were involved with which delivered successfully.

Q65: Now tell me a about a project you managed which failed to deliver.

Q66: We are considering introducing a new telephony solution. As a Call Centre Manager how would you see your role within the project team?

Q67: What are key milestones do you envisage leading up to its successful implementation?

Q68: What are the key features you would you look for in a new telephony system?

Tough Questions for All

Appendix I

Job Interview Scripts

These job interview scripts have been used to recruit Customer Services employees across a broad range of industries including banking, financial services, telecommunications, utilities and retail. You can use these to help prepare for your interview or to carry out a mock interview prior to the real thing. The more you prepare the better you will perform and we recommend that you formulate answers for each of the questions and practice as much as the timeframe will allow. By doing so, you will come across much more smoothly, naturally and confidently. In this section we include scripts for the most common Customer Service Jobs as follows:

Customer Services Advisor
Call Centre Agent
Customer Care Team Leader
Head of Customer Services

Customer Services Advisor
Assessment Sheet

Interviewer(s):
Date:
Candidate Name: _____

Punctuality:

Personal Presentation:

First Impression:

Score Summary

Key Competencies	Comment	Score (1-5)
Customer Handling		
Decision Making		
Negotiation skills		
Communication		
Team Working		
Planning and Organising		
Problem Solving		
Confidence		
Commitment		
Personality and Fit		
Initiative		
OVERALL		

Customer Services Advisor
Interview Script

Introduction:
Thank candidate for coming
Introduce interviewer
How was journey?
Did you have any problems finding or getting to the office?

Set the Scene:
Notify candidate of length of interview
Inform of due process
Who they will see next
Background to the company and the role

Exploration (Allow 45minutes)

Tell me about yourself. (Q1)

Comment	Score (1-5)

Talk me through your career progress to date (Q74)

Comment	Score (1-5)

I see from your CV you are currently employed by _____. Can you talk in more detail about your responsibilities in this job?

Comment	Score (1-5)

Why do you want to leave and what is it that attracts you about this Customer Services Advisor Role? (Q2)(Q9)

Comment	Score (1-5)

Can you give me an example of a time when you experienced good customer service and explain why it was good? (Q11)

Comment	Score (1-5)

Now tell me about a time when you actually gave effective customer service. (Q12)

Comment	Score (1-5)

Communication skills are very important in this role. Can you tell me about a time when you used your communication skills effectively? (Q16)

Comment	Score (1-5)

If you had to choose between writing to a customer or telephoning them, which would you favour? (Q19)

Comment	Score (1-5)

So what can you bring to the role of Customer Services Advisor? (Q6)

Comment	Score (1-5)

Talk me through an achievement on your CV or a time when you used these skills effectively when dealing with a customer. (Q81)

Comment	Score (1-5)

What would you say is the most difficult aspect of dealing with customers and how have you dealt with it? (Q13)

Comment	Score (1-5)

You will be part of a small team of 15 advisors. Can you describe your team working skills and give an example of when these worked well. (26)

Comment	Score (1-5)

What role do you generally play in team situations? (Q27)

Comment	Score (1-5)

Working in customer services what types of problems do you resolve in a daily basis? (Q32)

Comment	Score (1-5)

What do you like most about a career in Customer Services? (Q5)

Comment	Score (1-5)

Why did you choose to apply to our company, what was it that attracted you? (Q49)

Comment	Score (1-5)

What would you say is a reasonable time to spend in a Customer Services Advisor Role before moving on? (Q51)

Comment	Score (1-5)

Are you ambitious? Would you like to be a Team Leader or Supervisor one day? (Q52)

Comment	Score (1-5)

What other roles have you considered and why? (Q86)

Comment	Score (1-5)

If you don't get this job what will you do? (Q88)

Comment	Score (1-5)

What do you like to do outside of work? (Q89)

Comment	Score (1-5)

Closure Questions:

Can we check references?
Do you have any holidays booked?
What is your notice period?
Thank you for coming in. Based on what you have heard so far, how do you feel about the job?

Do you have any questions? (Make note of questions asked)

Comment	Score (1-5)

Thank candidate for coming and advise when they will hear of decision

End of Interview

Call Centre Agent
Assessment Sheet

Interviewer(s):
Date:
Candidate Name: _____

Punctuality:

Personal Presentation:

(Note data protection)

First Impression:

Score Summary

Key Competencies	Comment	Score (1-5)
Customer Handling		
Decision Making		
Negotiation skills		
Communication		
Team Working		
Planning and Organising		
Problem Solving		
Confidence		
Commitment		
Personality and Fit		
Initiative		
OVERALL		

Call Centre Agent
Interview Script

Introduction:
Thank candidate for coming
Introduce interviewer
How was journey?
Did you have any problems finding or getting to the office?

Set the Scene:
Notify candidate of length of interview
Inform of due process
Who they will see next
Background to the company and the role

Exploration (Allow 45minutes)

Give me a brief overview of your career to date (Q74)

Comment	Score (1-5)

Why should we select you, what will you bring to the role of Call Centre Agent? (Q6)

Comment	Score (1-5)

Talk me through your current job in more detail. Tell me about what you like and dislike? (Q5)

Comment	Score (1-5)

Why do you want to leave and why did you apply for this particular role ? (Q2)

Comment	Score (1-5)

Can you give me an example of a time when you experienced good customer service and explain why it was good? (Q11)

Comment	Score (1-5)

Now tell me about a time when you actually gave effective customer service. (Q12)

Comment	Score (1-5)

Communication skills are very important in this role. Can you tell me about a time when you used your communication skills effectively? (Q16)

Comment	Score (1-5)

Which telephony and IT systems are you familiar with?

Comment	Score (1-5)

Part of this role will involve dealing with angry customers. How would you respond to this type of call? (Q14)

Comment	Score (1-5)

How would you go about persuading a customer that our product was better than any other? (Q38)

Comment	Score (1-5)

There is a lot of variety on this role and some tasks can be difficult. What types of problems do you resolve on a daily basis in your current role? (Q32)

Comment	Score (1-5)

How did your last performance appraisal go and where do you think you could improve? (Q79)

Comment	Score (1-5)

Are you planning any further studies or education and where do you see yourself in 5 or 10 years time? (Q7)

Comment	Score (1-5)

Working in customer services can be stressful for many people. Tell me about a time you experience stress in your current job. (Q44)

Comment	Score (1-5)

How did you get on with your managers? (Q48)

Comment	Score (1-5)

Why did you choose to apply to our company, what was it that attracted you? (Q49)

Comment	Score (1-5)

Is see from your resume that you have moved jobs a lot over the past few years. Why is that and why do you think this one will be different? (Q51)

Comment	Score (1-5)

Are you ambitious? Would you like to be a Team Leader or Supervisor one day? (Q52)

Comment	Score (1-5)

How would you describe your personality?

Comment	Score (1-5)

Closure Questions:

Can we check references?
Do you have any holidays booked?
What is your notice period?
Thank you for coming in. Based on what you have heard so far, how do you feel about the job?

Do you have any questions? (Make note of questions asked)

Comment	Score (1-5)

Thank candidate for coming and advise when they will hear of decision

End of Interview

Customer Care Team Leader
Assessment Sheet

Interviewer(s):
Date:
Candidate Name: _____

Punctuality:

Personal Presentation:

(Note data protection)

First Impression:

Score Summary

Key Competencies	Comment	Score (1-5)
Communication		
Leadership		
Management		
Customer Service		
Decision Making		
Negotiation skills		
Team Working		
Planning and Organising		
Persuading and Influencing		
Confidence		
Commitment		
Personality and Fit		
IT and Data Analysis		
Productivity		
OVERALL		

Customer Care Team Leader
Interview Script

Introduction:
Thank candidate for coming
Introduce interviewer
How was journey?
Any problems finding or getting to the office?

Set the Scene:
Notify candidate of length of interview
Inform of due process
Who they will see next
Background to the company and the role

Exploration (Allow 45minutes)

Talk me through your CV and the relevant experience with leading teams (Q1)(Q74)

How would you describe your management style (Q48)

Comment	Score (1-5)

Talk me through your current job in more detail. Tell me about the daily challenges you face. (Q5)(Q61)

Comment	Score (1-5)

This role can be very demanding and some situations can be difficult to deal with. Can you tell me about a difficult situation you had to resolve recently (Q31)

Comment	Score (1-5)

Now tell me about a situation which did not work out as you would have wished. (Q33)

Comment	Score (1-5)

When recruiting customer care agents what characteristics and qualities do you look for? (Q15)

Comment	Score (1-5)

How do you get the best from your agents? What methods do you use? (Q55)

Comment	Score (1-5)

Describe a difficult situation you had with an underperforming employee and how did you resolve it? (Q59/60)

Comment	Score (1-5)

Communication skills are very important in this role. Can you tell me about a time when you used your communication skills effectively? (Q16)

Comment	Score (1-5)

What IT systems do you use to monitor and track performance and productivity? (Q63)

Comment	Score (1-5)

I see from your resume you were involved with the implementation of a new telephony system at _____. Tell me about the part you played in that.

Comment	Score (1-5)

Have you ever managed a project before? Is that something you would like to do in the future? (Q64)

Comment	Score (1-5)

Are you happy with your career progress to date? What would you change if you had the chance (Q75)

Comment	Score (1-5)

What do you know about our company? (Q8)

Comment	Score (1-5)

What is your view of flexible working and how would you approach the situation if one of your team requested a career break? (Q91)

Comment	Score (1-5)

What for you, is the most difficult aspect of being a Team Leader? (Q61)

Comment	Score (1-5)

How do you see your long term career plans in Customer Services? (Q53)

Comment	Score (1-5)

Closure Questions:

Can we check references?
Do you have any holidays booked?
What is your notice period?
Thank you for coming in. Based on what you have heard so far, how do you feel about the job?

Do you have any questions? (Make note of questions asked)

Comment	Score (1-5)

**Thank candidate for coming and advise when they will hear of decision
End of Interview**

Head of Customer Services
Assessment Sheet

Interviewer(s):
Date:
Candidate Name: _____

Punctuality:

Personal Presentation:

(Note data protection)

First Impression:

Score Summary

Key Competencies	Comment	Score (1-5)
Leadership		
Project Management		
Cost Management		
Communication		
Customer Service		
Decision Making		
Negotiation skills		
Planning and Organising		
Persuading and Influencing		
IT and telephony architecture awareness		
Business Analysis		
Industry Awareness		
OVERALL		

Head of Customer Services
Interview Script

Introduction:
Thank candidate for coming
Introduce interviewer

Set the Scene:
Notify candidate of length of interview
Inform of due process
Who they will see next
Background to the company and the role

Exploration (Allow 45minutes)

Talk me through your career progress to date (Q74)

Comment	Score (1-5)

What would you say is your greatest achievement? Tell me more about this and how it relates to this job. (Q81)

Comment	Score (1-5)

Given a chance what would you do differently in your career (Q75)

Comment	Score (1-5)

What can your bring to the role of Head of Customer Services? (Q43)

Comment	Score (1-5)

What do you see as being the greatest challenges to the Customer Servicing Industry and how best should a company such as ours meet and overcome them? (Q73)

Comment	Score (1-5)

Tell me about a change management project you were involved with which was targeted with improving productivity or increasing revenue. (Q64)

Comment	Score (1-5)

Now tell me about a project you managed which failed to deliver (Q65)

Comment	Score (1-5)

We are considering introducing a new telephony system. How would you see your role within the project team? (Q66)

Comment	Score (1-5)

How would you plan for such a project and what key milestones would you put in place? (Q67)

Comment	Score (1-5)

Getting and keeping top quality staff is always a challenge in customer services. What policies have you put in place to increase morale and how would you go about minimising staff turnover in your department?(Q69)

Comment	Score (1-5)

What size of teams and budgets did you manage in your last job and tell me about the challenges you have staying within the budget? (Q70)

Comment	Score (1-5)

I see from your resume you were made redundant from _____. Tell me about the circumstances relating to this. (Q77)

Comment	Score (1-5)

So, you had spent 14 years with them. We maintain a fast paced and dynamic environment here; how do you see yourself fitting in and adapting? (Q76)

Comment	Score (1-5)

Closure Questions:

Can we check references?
Do you have any holidays booked?
What is your notice period?
Thank you for coming in. Based on what you have heard so far, how do you feel about the job?

Do you have any questions? (Make note of questions asked)

Comment	Score (1-5)

Thank candidate for coming and advise when they will hear of decision.

End of Interview

Printed in the United Kingdom
by Lightning Source UK Ltd.
115075UKS00001B/40